You can influence from anywhere in your salon. Influencing doesn't require a title: It only requires certain thinking, behavior, and skills. Acquire them and you can lead an entire salon, an artistic vision, education, customer service—or just a better way to do your own consultations. *Leave Your Mark* is a book about influencing as a leader for salon owners, stylists, and other salon professionals. It represents my lifetime of experience, study, leading, and professional speaking. My aim is to help you leave your mark in the world and with the people around you.

The purpose of this book is to convince you that leaving your mark is the most important thing you will ever do. Each chapter is designed to help you achieve that by providing you with new thinking, behaviors, and people skills you'll need.

"I am here to shift your thinking."

Let the first shift be this: It's not what you are born with that matters. It's what you do with it. Together we can unleash the possibilities already inside you to surprise the world.

"You will be the same person in five years as you are today except for the people you meet and the books you read."

–CHARLIE "TREMENDOUS" JONES

Table of
CONTENTS

SHOUT OUTS

I want to give a shout out to a few of the people who supported me, encouraged me, and collaborated on this book. No one shoulders such an undertaking alone and I am no exception. Without love, creativity, and help from many people, my dream to leave my mark– by helping others leave theirs–would never have come together in these pages. I will be eternally grateful to those who helped me. Please let me introduce you to them. Who knows? They may be able to help you too!

GOD: Someone infinitely worthy to believe in.
STATUS: *Available.*

MONIQUE WILLIAMS: Someone who steadfastly believes in me more than I believe in myself.
STATUS: *Taken.*

JIM LUCAS: Someone who was brilliant in helping me write this book, could write his own book, and who displayed an amazing capacity to organize my random thoughts with incredible patience.
STATUS: *Available (until I write my next book).*

TOM VOLK: Someone who gives me unconditional support, challenges my thinking, lets me know when I'm right–and lets me know when I have the opportunity to be right in a different way. He is my Best Friend.
STATUS: *Taken.*

CECELIA DURDEN: Someone who knows the human dynamic and embraces it in a way that constantly reinforces my belief that the human heart is unstoppable. She is my sister and my psychologist; she always supports me, and constantly reminds me I should be charging more!

STATUS: *Taken (as a sister). Available (for therapy).*

JOSH HAFETZ: Someone who leaves his mark with every person he meets with ease and grace. He is a worthy role model, good friend, and a fantastic business partner who leads at the highest level.

STATUS: *Available as role model and mentor.*

HOWARD HAFETZ: Someone who gave me a stage and an audience. I am eternally grateful.

STATUS: *Available and always open for business.*

INTRODUCTION

> *Some will leave their mark.*
> *Some will be marked.*
> *Some will leave someone else's mark.*

I grew up in Los Angeles in a lower-income neighborhood. When I was 14 my best friend Robert lived in the apartment next door. One day his dad told us how to start our own business with only a bucket of water, vinegar, a squeegee, and some newspaper. Before we could say, "We don't do windows!" he gave us some vinegar and sent us out to comb the 200 units in our complex for customers. Before summer ended we had about $2,000.00 to split between us, as well as a regular job cleaning an elderly couple's apartment for $25.00 a week. Dick and Marge turned out to be great people and good friends. They left us a key to their place, gave us food to eat, and provided plenty of conversation. Marge especially enjoyed telling her stories with lots of color and detail. Dick would often smile and say, "Ask Marge the time and she'll tell you how to make a watch." Even though he teased her about it, I always enjoyed Marge's stories.

Several years later I met Monique, who is still the love of my life. I noticed that unlike Marge, Monique gets to the point very quickly. In fact, one of her favorite sayings is, "Just give me the net-net." What does net-net mean? Well, think of your own paycheck; there is the larger dollar amount at the top and then there is the smaller amount at the bottom after all your deductions. That's the net-net number—and it's the one that counts—because that's the money you can actually take to the bank. Compared with Marge, Monique's way of communicating is succinct. She's more about the meaning and results than detailed stories. I've really come to admire her style and it's the one I try to emulate in conversation and in writing this book. With each turn of the page I'll do my best to get to the point as quickly and succinctly as possible. There are many valuable books about business, self-improvement, and leadership. Like this one, there are insights and practices for any leader in any industry including doctors, lawyers, retail, technology, etc. My vision is to offer something important, do it in less than two hundred pages, and to give you real information that you can make part of your life one chapter at a time. I know your salon and your other roles keep you very busy. I figure, if you're going to invest your time, the least I can do is get to the point in a way that is easy, interesting, useful—and if I do it right—even a little entertaining.

Leave Your Mark is a not a management book. This is a book about leadership for salon owners, stylists, and other salon professionals. It represents my lifetime of experience, study, leading, and professional speaking. My aim is to help you leave your mark in your world and with the people around you.

The purpose of this book is to convince you that leaving your mark is the most important thing you will ever do. Each chapter is designed to help you achieve it by providing you with new thinking, behaviors, and people skills you'll need.

The value of this book is very bold—and this is why I think it is well worth your time:

| *I am here to shift your thinking.*

My intent is not to create some catchy new theory or to write a dissertation on psychology, personal growth, or leadership. I am here to challenge you, to guide you, and to expose you to different thinking. I encourage you to go deeper. Most of all I am here to help you get the most out of your personal and professional life.

Studies show that 90% of readers abandon books after the first chapter. That's why our first chapter, "Leave Your Mark" is first! If I have the opportunity to shift your thinking in just one way, it would be to focus you on leaving your mark. (Hmmm. I wonder how many people read introductions? Oh well.) With that said, let's go on to our first chapter. Take a quick break to check your texts, grab a snack, and repost some videos that popped up in your feed. I'll see you back here in two minutes!

LEAVE YOUR MARK

You make your mark by being true to who you are.

KAT GRAHAM

CHAPTER 1

WHAT EVERYONE WANTS

I grew up in a bi-racial household in Los Angeles with three siblings from different fathers. My mother's second marriage produced two children who I love, like, and admire deeply. My sister's name is Cecelia and my brother is Julian. Cece is an incredible role model and an inspiration in more ways than she knows. Jules has created a unique and completely authentic life with a lightness of being and a knack for approaching the world on his own terms. I value our close relationships, and before continuing my story, I wanted to give them a shout out because they are such a positive part of my life.

I took a city bus each day from my mostly African American neighborhood in L.A. to the nearby city of Gardena, which was predominantly Asian. Needless to say, my unstable home life, new stepfather, new neighborhood, and now my new school, didn't exactly foster a clear sense of identity in my already hormonal teenage brain. Without taking you through all the detail, let's just say that by the end of high school I had attended four schools in four years—and I didn't end up with many yearbook signatures.

At 16, when I left home for good, I didn't have much of anything figured out. Yet, over time my blended upbringing, the diversity of neighborhood, and my cross-cultural school experiences somehow managed to give me a good understanding of myself and others. I learned firsthand that people who may seem different at first are exactly the same in the ways that really matter.

> *"We all want significance, self-worth, and a sense of belonging"*
> -STAN SLAP

What I found out, and what I want to share with you, is that everyone: You, your parents, your friends (and even the Kardashians) all want the same thing. We want to leave our mark. We may not be searching for, "The meaning of life," but we are all searching for, "Meaning in our lives." The net-net is that we all want our lives to count. We all want to have a purpose, and a benefit, for our time on Earth. We want to know that our being here makes a difference.

COUNT TO TEN

You've probably heard someone say, "Take a deep breath and count to ten," as a way to gather yourself before reacting in haste. Well, that's great advice and it illustrates another lesson I learned early in life.

> *"It's not what happens to you that defines you.*
> *It's how you respond to it"*
> -EPICTETUS

Even though my upbringing may have been, let's say unusual, my experiences instilled in me a strong set of values—even though I wasn't able to articulate them at the time. What some might see as a difficult childhood (and great material for stand-up comedy) I choose to see as a rich learning experience. They created my thinking, my worldview, and the values I hold dear. They are what drive me to leave my mark. Adversity did not define my character. *Adversity exposed my character.*[1] In the same circumstances, I could have lost myself, pretended to be someone I'm not, or I could have been marked by stronger personalities. Instead, my choice was to use my situation as a catalyst to define my own mark. Now, I invite you to begin making your own choices.

Whether your life has been "unusual" or completely awesome, none of us avoids adversity completely. We each walk our own path and we've all gotten a couple bumps, bruises, and scraped knees. As you consider your life experience, whether it's your childhood, education, finances, relationships, or your zip code, ask yourself, "Have my experiences defined me?" or "Do my choices define me?"

I'LL BET YOU CAN RELATE

In the Introduction I said the purpose of this book is to convince you that leaving your mark is the most important thing you will ever do. Maybe you grew up like I did or you knew someone like me in high school. Maybe you had it better or maybe you had it worse (God bless you). Regardless of your experience I'm guessing you can relate and the desire to leave your mark is something you already feel deep inside—even if you've never put it into words until now. However, if you really do need convincing that leaving your mark is the most important thing you will ever do, I wouldn't invoke Gandhi, JFK, Henry David Thoreau, or Ralph Waldo Emerson. What I would say is this. Whether you're trying to or not *you are already leaving your mark*. The things you believe, the things you say and do, and your impact (or lack of impact) on others is already speaking for you. The larger point is that it is possible to exert control over the mark you leave so that you will be proud and so others will value what you bring to the table.

> *"I never said to be like me. I say, be yourself and make a difference."*
> **-MARILYN MANSON**

CHOOSE YOUR MARK

There is a Chinese proverb, "The best time to plant a tree is 20 years ago. The second best time is now." So, it's not too late if you're older and it's not too early if you're just starting out. Just ask yourself, "What kind of mark am I already leaving and what kind of mark do I really want to leave?" As you think about that question in all its awesomeness, I'll lay out the basic principles that should guide you as you choose your mark.

1. Do you want to be remembered for what you took or for what you gave?
2. Is your mark something compelling that others will follow?

My own observation, and what I know to be true, is that we all have the potential to lead. The trick as salon owners or business people of any kind is that you are only leading if you have followers. They say, "If people follow you, you are a leader. If no one is following you, you're just someone out taking a walk." Your team will only follow you—and go the extra mile—when you give them a way to grow, bring meaning to their lives, and help them make a difference too.

WHAT SUCCESS LOOKS LIKE

You are unique and I sincerely hope your mark will be too. To be clear, as you choose your mark the most important thing is for it to be truly and authentically yours. To be compelling, enduring, and to inspire others to take action, your mark must also:

- Leave people better off than you found them
- Build up their significance, self-worth, and sense of belonging
- Elevate humanity
- Allow you to live by your values.

NOW WHAT?

The context for this book is the business world. The ideas and information it contains were chosen to satisfy my desire to leave my mark in the business world and specifically with you as a business owner or leader. In my study of leaders, one common trait I've documented is how the great ones are the same at home as they are at work. In other words, the values they live by at work are the same ones they live by at home. These leaders are consistent, always the same person, and always authentic. It will make me smile if you read something here you can also apply to your personal life, your spiritual life, your volunteer pursuits, or your role in someone else's life. For now, however, let's take our new understanding about why we each need to leave our mark and turn our attention to how to do it with intent and passion in our roles as kick-ass business leaders.

EXERCISE

Fill this out in pencil so you can refine and evolve your answers over time.

On a scale from 1-10 where 1 is *not at all* and 10 is *killing it*, **How well are you currently leaving your mark?**
(Low)   (High)

1   2   3   4   5   6   7   8   9   10

How would you describe the mark you are currently leaving?

_____
_____
_____
_____

What would you prefer your mark to be?

_____
_____
_____
_____

How well are you leaving your preferred mark?

(Low)   (High)

1   2   3   4   5   6   7   8   9   10

Come back to this exercise after reading this book, and then again after one month, after three months, and after one year. How have your answers and your ability to leave your mark improved?

CAN I BUY A VALUE?

Values are like fingerprints. Nobody's are the same
but you leave 'em all over everything you do.

ELVIS

In my middle school, fashion and social status were largely based on your sneakers and how you dressed. One day, as I stood up from my regular lunch table in eighth grade, I didn't notice someone had dropped a packet of ketchup on the cafeteria floor. With my luck, I accidentally stepped on it and what happened next was right out of one of those Hollywood "teenage angst" movies. My foot popped the packet and ketchup shot all over not one but four of the most popular kids in school. I wasn't exactly in the "Top Ten" in my middle school so I already knew what was coming. There was an instant silence as the four of them stood up and at the top of their voices for all to hear, humiliated me in front of everyone. They told me I was a jackass and I was lucky they didn't beat me senseless. They said that by the next day I'd better show up with enough money to replace their stuff if the ketchup didn't come out. Honestly, I did appreciate the option to buy my way out of an ass whoopin' but any dreams I may have had to be one of the cool kids vanished in an instant. Fortunately, the lunch bell rang and everyone went on to class. I walked alone, taking the least-traveled route so I could just disappear.

Taking the long way made me late. When I arrived English class was already packed. I prepared for my little, "Walk of shame" but to my surprise, nothing was said. It was like any other day and the Ketchup Incident never happened. Two days later, I found out from my friend Steve that Marian Barnes (the most popular girl in school) told my entire English class not to say a word about what happened in the lunchroom. In that moment I realized that I valued loyalty. Her loyalty to me was unexpected, and unearned, but for some reason she offered it unconditionally. She instantly gave me self worth and made me feel safe. To this day I am fiercely loyal to my friends and family (sometimes to a fault) and I only surround myself with people who are fiercely loyal to me. You see, loyalty still gives me the same thing it did all those years ago when Marian Barnes stood up for me. It gives me significance, self-worth, and a sense of belonging—a topic we'll discuss in depth in Chapter Four.

Marian gave me an important gift. She not only offered me her loyalty, she helped me recognize and name loyalty as one of my values—and I've felt connected to her ever since. At other times in life people have done the opposite. Instead of giving me their loyalty they withheld it. I've experienced the lack of loyalty in my work life, home life, and in my community. I've quit a job, ended a friendship, and left a charitable cause because of it. If there were ever anything to cause me to disconnect mentally, physically, and emotionally it's when you step on one of my values.

Marian left her mark with me that day. Even now we still keep in touch. I have shared the story with her on more than one occasion and, interestingly enough, she doesn't remember that day. Not because it wasn't important but because loyalty is also one of her values. To her it was just a natural thing to do. Loyalty defines her. It's how she lives her life. It's one of the filters she uses to make decisions. That day she did not think about what she did. She made the decision swiftly and instinctively. That's how values work. And by being herself, she earned my enduring emotional commitment.

WHY VALUES?

> *"When your values are clear to you, making decisions becomes easier."*
> -ROY E. DISNEY

Wouldn't it be an amazing gift if someone came to you and said, "I have a gift for you. This gift will help you know yourself, be yourself, and give you the strength and confidence to live your truth. In fact, if there is a 'secret' to life, this is it"? It is perfectly human to search for meaning in life, to be uncertain, and to wonder if our lives will ever be something we'll be proud of. Since life doesn't come with an owner's manual we each do our best and life happens. Some of us get lucky. Some of us question our self-worth. And, some of us just go along without really examining our lives or how we're living. Regardless, the one thing we can all use, and the gift I'm about to give you, are the answers to three questions,

- "Who am I?"
- "How should I live my life?"
- "Will my life matter?"

> *Values define us. They are the key to what we love, what we hate, what rewards us and robs us. Values are what make us happy or sad and guide our decisions whether we are conscious of them or not.*

That is why values are important and why you need to discover yours.

DEFINE VALUES

Just so we know what we're talking about, my definition for values is

> *Values are the standards and principles that guide our actions and beliefs.*

Values define what is good and worthwhile for you. They reveal how you make decisions and how you actually live your life.

> *Core values are the core of who you are as a person.*

Core values are those you would **fight for, quit a job over, or leave a friendship to protect.**

To help me explain, let's take my value for education as an example. It's something that gives me focus and direction and it levels the playing field for me. In this beauty business, education is probably one of your values too. I have a friend named Suzanne and it turns out she doesn't really value education. Even though we don't value the exact same things, it's easy to be friends with Suzanne. We have a lot of other things in common and I've decided I can overlook our differences on education. On the other hand, Claire is a former friend who did not share my value for authenticity and it used to crop up in our friendship all the time. Authenticity is not just one of my values, it's one of my *core values*. It's something that defines me and is at the center of who I am in the world. Unlike my relationship with Suzanne where I could flex, I ultimately could not overlook Claire's inability to be authentic with me. Not only was it difficult to know "Which Claire" I was talking to at any moment, our relationship became sandpaper to my soul because her disregard for authenticity made me feel unsafe to the point where I had to leave the friendship.

I can recite several more of my values on a moment's notice but my core values are authenticity, family, and respect. These are the three I use to identify myself to the world and the ones I want the world to know me by. Telling people my values certainly reveals more about me than telling them my name. Along the same lines, I have always tried to convince salon owners to include their employee's core values on their nametags. Imagine if I were your stylist and my nametag displayed my three core values:

What if your staff had nametags that included?

ADOPT OR DISCOVER?

I hope you're thinking, "OK, I get it. Now, how can I find out which values are mine?"

I often ask people to write down their top three values in 30 seconds. What I've seen is that only about one-out-of-fifteen can do it. And when they do, about 50% of the time things they write down are not values by our definition. Even more troubling is the other 50% are not values they actually hold but, rather, things they thought would sound good or that they aspire to.

The reason this happens is because it isn't common for us to explicitly talk about our values, therefore we're not very good at it. People also tend to state their *aspirations* rather than their actual values. If you're describing the values you think you ought to have, or you wish you had, you're probably not being authentic and people will notice because your actions will not match your words. In other words, you may talk the talk but you're not walking the walk.

After about age 21, most if not all, of our values have been formed.[2] As we grow up our values are formed based on our relationships and our experiences. Here are the people who most often shape our values.

- Ages 0-7   Parents
- Ages 8-13   Teachers, heroes, role models
- Ages 14-20   Friends and peers
- Ages 21+   Values are mostly established and then tested from time-to-time.

Unless you're still a teenager it's very likely your values are already formed. Since this is generally the case, it's much more useful to think about our values as something we discover—rather than something we actively define or create. In other words, you already have your values. Now let's figure out what they are.

LIST-O-VALUES

To kick-start our process I've chosen a list of 50 values from over 4,000 possibilities. After we work through this, you're welcome to examine longer lists and to reflect on other values that are true for you—even those not captured on anyone else's list.

What I'd like you to do is go through the list on the next page and put a check mark in each box to the right.

NO.	VALUE	YES	MAYBE	NO
1	Achievement	☐	☐	☐
2	Affection	☐	☐	☐
3	Ambition	☐	☐	☐
4	Art/artistry	☐	☐	☐
5	Balance	☐	☐	☐
6	Caring	☐	☐	☐
7	Collaboration	☐	☐	☐
8	Commitment	☐	☐	☐
9	Communication	☐	☐	☐
10	Community	☐	☐	☐
11	Competence	☐	☐	☐
12	Continuous learning	☐	☐	☐
13	Cooperation	☐	☐	☐
14	Creativity	☐	☐	☐
15	Efficiency	☐	☐	☐
16	Excellence	☐	☐	☐
17	Fairness	☐	☐	☐
18	Family	☐	☐	☐
19	Financial Security	☐	☐	☐
20	Forgiveness	☐	☐	☐
21	Friendship	☐	☐	☐
22	Generosity	☐	☐	☐
23	Growth	☐	☐	☐
24	Harmony	☐	☐	☐
25	Health	☐	☐	☐

NO.	VALUE	YES	MAYBE	NO
26	Helpfulness	☐	☐	☐
27	Honesty	☐	☐	☐
28	Humility	☐	☐	☐
29	Humor/fun	☐	☐	☐
30	Independence	☐	☐	☐
31	Integrity	☐	☐	☐
32	Loyalty	☐	☐	☐
33	Making a difference	☐	☐	☐
34	Order	☐	☐	☐
35	Passion	☐	☐	☐
36	Patience	☐	☐	☐
37	Perseverance	☐	☐	☐
38	Personal growth	☐	☐	☐
39	Power	☐	☐	☐
40	Recognition	☐	☐	☐
41	Reliability	☐	☐	☐
42	Respect	☐	☐	☐
43	Responsibility	☐	☐	☐
44	Risk taking	☐	☐	☐
45	Spirituality	☐	☐	☐
46	Success	☐	☐	☐
47	Teaching	☐	☐	☐
48	Transparency	☐	☐	☐
49	Trust	☐	☐	☐
50	Wisdom	☐	☐	☐

YOUR OWN LIST OF VALUES

Now let's get down to business. Discovering your values involves a few steps (and maybe even several attempts) but together we're going to make it happen. First, go back to our last exercise and look for the values you marked "Yes." From that list, pick your top 10 and place them below in the next table. If you have values not listed in the 50 above, feel free to write them down. I considered providing definitions for these 50 values but I realized it would be better if you wrote your own definitions. The point is for your values and definitions to make sense to you.

NO.	VALUE	DEFINITION
1		
2		
3		
4		
5		
6		
7		
8		
9		
10		

YOUR SHORT LIST OF VALUES

It's hard to remember 20, 30, or 40 values but, in my experience, most people can remember five. Now what I'd like you to do is select your most important five values and write them below. This is getting kinda serious so be thoughtful about your Top Five. These will be the five you can remember and recite to anyone who asks. Don't worry. The values that don't make the Top Five are still your values; it's just that these five rank higher.

NO.	VALUE	DEFINITION
1		
2		
3		
4		
5		

YOUR CORE VALUES

Our final step is to examine your Top Five values for the three that really define you as a person. Remember, core values are those you would **fight for, quit a job, or leave a friendship over.** You know by now the core values that define me are: Authenticity, family, and respect. What defines you?

THE CORE VALUES THAT TRULY DEFINE ME

NO.	VALUE	DEFINITION
1		
2		
3		

THE BENEFIT OF MY CORE VALUES

> *It turns out that the benefits our values give us are more important than the values themselves.*

Now, I admit this is taking some effort! We're almost where we need to be. Hang in there for just one more step.

Please write your core values in the first column of the following table and copy your definitions for your core values into the second column. In the final column, I want you to write down the benefit your core values give you.

It's important to get this step right. To make it easier, I'll give you my example and then provide space for you to follow through.

EXAMPLE

VALUE	DEFINITION	BENEFIT
Family	Unconditional love Support, Community, Caring	Security, Predictability, Comfort, Significance, Self-worth, Sense of belonging
Respect	Kind, Generous Acknowledging, Validating	Confidence, Peace, Happiness, Significance, Self-worth, Sense of belonging
Authenticity	Open, Honest, On-time communication	Clarity, Hope, Focus, Significance, Self-worth, Sense of belonging

Notice how each of my values has a different name and how the definition for each value is unique. Now, look what's happening in a few cases in the column labeled "Benefit." There are some repeats. So, when you get right down to it, many of our values give us the same, or similar, benefits.

Now, you try it.

THE BENEFITS OF MY CORE VALUES

VALUE	DEFINITION	BENEFIT

Usually we start conversations by identifying our differences. Imagine what your world would look like if you were to start every interaction by looking for things you have in common with the other person and building from there. How much more productive could you be? Your new knowledge, that different values may hold similar benefits, will be a tremendous help in getting along with people and leading teams—especially when everyone's values don't match 100%. Using the benefits our values provide each of us as individuals is the key to discovering our common humanity and mutual interests. Luckily, that is the subject of the next chapter. See you there!

WALK THE WALK

If you don't stick to your values when they're being tested, they're not values they're hobbies.

JON STEWART

Once in a while I get together with some of my "guy friends" for dinner. One evening we were talking about the difference between our personal and professional lives. Most of the guys felt like they could be their natural Christian selves at home but that they had to be jerks at work in order to be good leaders.

That seemed strange to me so I asked, "What are you struggling with? Being nice or being a jerk?"

When I lead workshops it's common for people to say, "I am one person at work and another person at home." My response is always, "I believe you are one person. So, when you aren't feeling unified

- Which place is not getting the authentic you?
- In which place you are core values being violated?
- In which place are you emotionally connected and emotionally disconnected?

Many of us feel like we cannot live by our own values when ours are not the same ones our bosses, colleagues, or even our spouses have.

In an informal survey of 10,000 managers the top two values listed were family and integrity. Ironically, these were also the top two values they reported that their work violated on a daily basis. These managers felt like they had to leave their values at home. What happens when you abandon your values? The amygdala, the part of your brain that controls your emotions, switches to the "off" position and emotionally disengages from what you're doing. This happens no matter if you abandon your values at work, home, or play.

So, how can you be true to yourself and your values and reconcile the difference between your values and the values of the people around you? In other words,

How do we use values to find common ground?

The secret is what we talked about toward the end of the last chapter. We start by discovering our own values, listing them, creating our short list and definitions, and then arriving at our core values. That is truly a great start. However, it's only when we **define what our values mean to us, and discover how they benefit us**, that we are able to begin the process of finding common ground with others. Even though different people have different values, the benefits associated with those values are a universal language that is understood and accepted by everyone.

> *It's not the value itself that is important.*
> *What is important is*
> *what your value gives you or enables*
> *for you.*

COMMON GROUND

They say, "Never talk religion or politics," but let's run with the scissors and use religion to show how people can find common ground. Let's say you have a value of religion, if I respond that I'm an atheist—then we are off to a flying stop! However, if you speak in terms of the benefits your value of religion gives you (e.g., hope, direction, focus) and that when you experience those things you feel happy, centered, and significant then your story is going to resonate with me whether I have a value of religion or not. You see, if you have a value of religion and I have a value of education, when we concentrate on the benefits, (e.g., hope, direction, focus) we speak in a universal language that is understood and embraced by everyone. When we concentrate on the benefits of our values we focus on what we have in common instead of our differences. When we discover what we have in common we engage emotionally, regardless if our lists of values have the exact same names or not.

TYPES OF COMMITMENT

Ultimately, when my own values are met, I feel supported and safe—that is always the bottom line for me personally. Support and safety is at the core of everything we do as humans. We need these feelings in order to function. Not living our values, or having them violated by a spouse, boss, peers, kids, neighbors or friends, causes us to disconnect emotionally. You may be committed to someone (or something) financially, physically, and mentally—but if you're not committed on an emotional level you are leaving potential on the table. Of these four types of commitment, like my good friend Stan Slap[1] says,

> *"Emotional commitment is the ultimate trigger of stellar performance"*

Losing emotional commitment leads to dissatisfaction at work, undermined teams, under performance, people quitting—and even walkouts. Gaining emotional commitment is how we get our people to go "above and beyond" what's normally expected.

The loss of emotional commitment is destructive in relationships in ways that are easy to see and in some ways that are not so obvious. One of the hard to detect ways is what I call "Quitting and Staying." This happens when you lose the emotional commitment of an employee but she or he continues to show up at work everyday only to perform at the very minimum. Have your ever experienced that with a pair of shoes? You know, the ones that are not good enough to keep but not bad enough to get rid of? Employees can be like that. Minimum performance causes little problems at first but, if left unchecked, creates a negative spiral that impacts your clients, you, and the rest of your team, and sooner or later, your entire work culture.

WHAT EMOTIONAL COMMITMENT LOOKS LIKE

Your people show up to work (maybe even on time, or at least not *that late*). They do their job to a point where they are not bad enough to get rid of but certainly not good enough to keep. And, then they collect their paychecks. They don't come in early, don't show up for meetings, and won't consistently come to educational classes. What you're missing is that "little extra" performance that only comes with emotional commitment, and it's keeping you from transforming your good salon into a great salon. What can you do?

Here's what emotional commitment looks like:

- Staying late to accommodate a walk-in
- Coming for education on a day off
- Stylist and staff cleaning the salon because making payroll was tight this month
- Staying loyal to you after a walk-out
- Mentoring other employees with no thought of anything in return.

Unfortunately, you don't know if you have emotional commitment until you need it most. When you are already drowning is not the time to find out whether your team will throw you a life preserver.

BURNOUT

Employees aren't the only ones at risk of losing emotional commitment. In our hectic business world, salon owners themselves can lose emotional commitment to their cause. It usually happens when they lose sight of their values and why they started their salon in the first place. If you have forgotten why you started your salon you will start to disengage. Little things will start to slip at first—

like bathroom maintenance—and then big things start to happen —including losing focus on your client service. In the end, being behind your chair or leading your team is a grind and you burnout. I define burnout as,

> *When there is no emotional return on your physical investment.*

To avoid burnout, get back in touch with your own values on a regular basis—no less frequently than every three months. Remind yourself, not of *what you do*, but **why** do you what you do. If you lose your own emotional commitment you lose the drive to leave your mark.

YOUR JOB

I've met with thousands of salon owners over the years. There isn't a single "type" of successful salon owner. I've met petite ones, tall ones, mature ones, young ones, pretty ones and prettier ones. Some are surly and some are kind. Some are dead serious and some use humor to make their way along. The one thing all the successful ones have in common is they know their values. Their values define them. They define their businesses. They weave a common thread of vision their people find compelling enough to buy into. Rather than having employees who are only looking out for themselves, employees of good leaders say, "We're like family here. We support each other unconditionally, we do the right thing for the client and the salon, and we do the right thing for one another. This is *our* salon." The best way to achieve that is to create a salon whose people know and respect each other's values—and the benefits those values provide each individual.

You know from experience that a great salon environment and culture doesn't just happen. So, why does it happen in some salons and not in others? Here's why.

SHARED VALUES

Successful leaders not only know their own values *they know how to hire people who are willing to share their values with them.* We already know that not everyone has the same values. That's why we try to hire people who hold similar values, who seek similar benefits, and/or are willing, at the very least, not violate the organization's or fellow team members' values. Finally, we want to foster a values-driven culture that sets our people up to pursue the salon owner's vision and to be a part of something bigger than any one person.

YOU CAN'T MOTIVATE THEM

The number one question I'm asked is "How do I motivate my people?" I have great news for you! It's not your job as a leader to motivate your people. More than anything, your job is simply to not extinguish your people's motivation. Your job is to find out what motivates them, from the inside, and then satisfy those needs at work. I'll give you a hint: What motivates them is the same thing that motivates you—values. Great leaders, leaders who leave their mark, will explore and identify their followers' values.

The way you tap into someone's internal motivation, and gain their emotional commitment, is by honoring their values. Allowing your people to live their values 24/7 allows them to share a common cause with you. Needless to say, this is a difficult task for anyone. So, my advice is to start talking about values during the interview process.

> *If the first time you talk about values is at the six-month mark, during a difficult 1:1, it's probably too late.*

NEW EMPLOYEES AND NEW SALONS

Chances are, since you're reading this book, you already own a salon and have employees. That's why it's so important to get clarity around your values and the benefits they provide to you. You then compare them with the values of your current employees and start looking at how they match up. The fact is that you need to get the most out of everyone on your current team by going through this values-matching process. However,

> *What about the next employee you hire?*

Or, what if you are reading this book before you've even opened your own salon?

Great leaders have one thing in common. They know how to transform their values into a compelling cause for others to follow. Mother Teresa, Martin Luther King, Steve Jobs, Jesus, JFK all knew how. They communicated who they were, what they stood for, and where they were going. People were drawn to them and took up their causes—connecting themselves emotionally to their leader's values and vision. By mobilizing thousands, millions, and billions of people these leaders were able to leave an indelible mark that not one of them could have left by themselves.

You may not have the opportunity to hire everyone on your team from scratch—but what you can do is this:

> *Make values the centerpiece of every future hiring decision. Only hire those who are willing to support your values and fight for your cause.*

MAKE A DIFFERENCE TODAY

Learn the values of your people. Then you have the knowledge to earn their lasting emotional commitment. When I say your people, I include staff, clients, your kids, spouse, friends, and community members. I've worked with people from India to Indiana. People are all wired the same. What motivates us, what makes us the happiest, what makes us the most productive, what captures our emotional commitment is when our values are being met and the people around us support our values.

Having our values acknowledged and validated provides what Maslow articulated in his Hierarchy of Needs: significance, self–worth and sense of belonging. Come to think of it, that's a great segue to our next chapter!

EXERCISE

I urge you to share your values with your team, and to learn their values, with the goal of gaining their emotional commitment. Remember, when you know each other's values—and the benefits those values provide—you have what it takes to reach common ground and build a shared future together. Complete this activity with your staff within the next 14 calendar days.

I like to look at this as a What, When, Why, Who type of exercise. Here's what I mean.

- **What**. Have a group staff meeting (approximately 60-90 minutes) to introduce the concept of values. Present your values to your staff. Discuss them until everyone understands your values and the benefits your values give you personally. Explore the values and benefits that resonate with your team. As a follow up, spend at least 30 minutes during your next 1:1 with each staff member to discover their values and figure out the benefits their values provide them. Then match up the values and/or benefits you share in common.
- **When**. Do it at a staff meeting within 14 days from today.

Have all 1:1s complete within 30 days.

- **Why.** Sharing values gives my team something to believe in and lets us connect on a deeper level. Learning their values allows me to help them satisfy their needs at work and earn their emotional commitment.

- **Who.** First with your own management team. Then with your front desk people. Follow that with your stylists, assistants, and other staff. Find a partner (salon manager, friend, spouse, coach) who will hold you accountable to follow through on this task—and give that person permission to hold your feet to the fire! Partnering with someone to keep you on track is probably outside your comfort zone but it can be extremely effective. After all, you're only human and we all need a little reminder from time to time.

WHAT COMES
AFTER SEX?

Self-esteem is the reputation we acquire with ourselves.

NATHANIEL BRANDEN

I'd like to take you back to your childhood for just a moment to connect with something every one of us has experienced. Let's time-travel to elementary school and think about the playground at recess or during P.E. They say that school is for learning but it's also an important way we develop our social standing, sort ourselves into groups, and start to really form our self-image and our identity.

Remember how in kickball, or soccer, or softball, there were two captains and each captain chose their team from the group of kids? The same kids tended to get "picked first" and others tended to get "picked last." There may have even been kids that didn't get picked at all and eventually didn't bother showing up to play.

This kind of thing also happens in our adult lives. Have you ever been left out of a party invitation, excluded from an education team, rejected for a job, or had a client request another stylist instead of you? Yeah, that feels crappy. Oh well, what doesn't kill us makes us stronger, right?

BUT WHAT MAKES US HAPPY?

Back in the 1950's it was popular for psychologists to study what makes unhappy people unhappy. Then along came a man who decided to do the opposite. Abraham Maslow, an American psychologist, decided to study what makes happy people happy. He figured out that we don't get happy all at once. Instead, as humans we tend to satisfy our most basic needs first, like securing food, water, shelter, and sex before we start trying to satisfy more complex desires like being happy (Answering, of course, the question, "What comes after sex?") With 60 years of hindsight it seems pretty obvious that if aliens from outer space caused you to lose your house and all your possessions, your first step would not be to visit the nearest Lexus dealership. No, you would most likely reach a friend to see if you could stay with her (shelter). She would ask you if you're ok (safety) and she would offer you something to eat (food). After you settle down and start to make sense of what just happened, she would invite you to stay with her as long as you needed to (love/belonging). With her encouragement and support you would start feeling better. You'd begin to venture out, resume your usual routine and romantic life, go to your job, resume workouts, and participate in the other things that make you feel normal. Eventually you would move out and into your own home again (self-esteem). Finally, at an old age with your friends and family gathered around, you will tell your loved ones the story of how E.T. stole your house and took it back to planet Alfa 177. For the 1000th time you would lecture them on how you worked through it, got over it, and finally fulfilled your potential as an artist (self-actualization).

And so it is with what Abraham called his Hierarchy of Needs.

Intuitively, as it turns out, we need certain things to be constant and stable (like some kale in our salad and a pimped out crib) before we have much chance of being happy. It also turns out that our path to happiness is not a direct path from Point A to Point B. Even the most stable and happy people must loop through levels in Maslow's little triangle, constantly improving ourselves, evolving, and growing. As we work through Maslow's Hierarchy, whether we are aware of it or not, we develop what my friend Stan Slap calls, "Significance, self-worth, and a sense of belonging.[1]" In other words, we develop an understanding of how much we matter, how much we love ourselves, and where we belong in terms of place (like country, state, or home town) and in terms of relationships (like parents, friends, and profession).

NURTURING OTHERS

It's no surprise that significance, self-worth, and a sense of belonging can take a lifetime to buildup, but we can be setback—or even lose it—in a single moment. Imagine what your employee (or you) would feel like if he/she hears:

- You're not a team player
- Everyone else knew what I meant
- You were the only one who didn't finish
- You did a terrible job
- No one likes you
- Everybody did better than you
- You weren't chosen
- I prefer another stylist
- You're fired!

Holding high standards of performance, giving constructive feedback, and making difficult choices are part of leading your organization and developing your people. However, the message here is to carefully choose how you communicate when coaching people or giving them your feedback. Avoid the collateral damage that comes with using language that goes beyond what you intended. I say, "Be easy on the person and hard on the issue." As you clarify how you would like someone to perform, please take care not to diminish the other person's sense of significance, self-worth, and sense of belonging.

SIGNIFICANCE, SELF-WORTH, AND SENSE OF BELONGING

One of the most important parts of our early life development happened on that kickball playground in elementary school. Whether we were picked first or picked last (or stopped playing altogether so we could learn to code, live in our mom's basement, and hack (www.ashleymadison.com) we learned what it felt like to experience our own:

- Significance (does the world even know I'm alive?)
- Self-worth (do I value myself and do others value me too?)
- Sense of belonging (does anyone need me?)

Maslow stated that whatever people do we are driven to satisfy our need for significance, self-worth, and sense of belonging. In other words, when we're feeling positive about those things we feel happier and when we are feeling negative about those things we feel unhappier.

To make sure we agree on what we're talking about, here are the definitions we will be using throughout this book:

Significance: The quality of being important or having notable worth or influence.
Self-worth: Considering yourself to be a good person who deserves love and respect.
Sense of belonging: Feeling like a member, or a natural part, of a group.

IMPACT ON LEADERS

A traveler came upon three individuals working with stone. Curious about their work, the traveler approached the first worker and asked, "What are you doing?" Without the slightest hesitation, the worker replied, "I am a stone cutter and I am cutting stones." Wanting to know more, the traveler approached the second worker and asked the same question. To this, the second worker thought for a moment, gazed briefly at the traveler and explained, "I am a stone cutter and I am cutting stones to earn money to support my family." Fascinated by the two different responses, the traveler approached the third worker and asked, "What are you doing?" Stopping for a moment, the third worker stared at the stone in his hand, slowly turned to the traveler, and said, "I AM BUILDING A CATHEDRAL!"

In my work consulting with business owners all over the country, I help my clients understand their businesses in terms of:

- Products
- Processes, and
- People.

Time and time again, the wild card is people. And, you'll remember from our discussion of values, it is very difficult to get exceptional performance from people if you don't have their emotional commitment.

So, what does the story of the three stonecutters have to do with leaving your mark? In a way, it's self-explanatory. If you had a chance to hire one of these three, I'm guessing 100% of you would hire the one building a cathedral. It would be hard to find a better example of emotional commitment.

A significant part of leaving your mark is your ability to help, allow, and encourage your team to leave their marks. Again, think about yourself. When you feel that you're not leaving your mark, it's most often when you're not feeling good about your significance, self-worth, and sense of belonging. Lacking this, you feel less creative, less confident, less certain, etc. The people who make up your team are just like you. If you build up their significance, self-worth, and sense of belonging you have a chance to turn them from "stonecutters" into "cathedral builders."

HOW TO DO IT

You can believe me, or prove it to yourself, but building up significance, self-worth, and a sense of belonging in others boomerangs and makes you feel good too. It's a great example of instant karma. In fact, I hope you don't take my word for it because by doing it yourself you will be able to feel it as well as understand it.

So, how do you do that? You do it with your words and actions. If you want the physical, financial, and emotional commitment of your team—and the exceptional performance it provides to your business—make it your habit to offer your people the following encouragements every single day. In fact, on a scale of 1-to-10 take a few moments to rate yourself. How well are you encouraging your people right now? Note: 1 is "not at all" and 10 is "perfectly."

Continue to exercise on the next page.

MY TEAM

BEHAVIOR	1 = NOT AT ALL
	10 = PERFECTLY

Approval	☐
Acknowledgement	☐
Validation	☐
Asking rather than telling	☐
Complimenting	☐
Recommending rather than demanding	☐
Acceptance	☐
Collaboration	☐
Giving of yourself	☐
Respect	☐
Opportunities	☐
Growth	☐
Security	☐
Integrity	☐
Loyalty	☐
Inclusion	☐

EXERCISE

If you're willing to do a little extra credit, you can deepen your understanding of significance, self-worth, and sense of belonging by adding two steps to the exercise you just finished.

You just scored yourself on how well you encourage your team as a whole. Now, let's break it down. List out the name of every member of your team and score yourself again on how well you treat specific individuals. (I'll give you some writing space below. If you need more, use a separate sheet of paper.)

TEAM MEMBER _____

BEHAVIOR	1 = NOT AT ALL 10 = PERFECTLY
Approval	☐
Acknowledgement	☐
Validation	☐
Asking rather than telling	☐
Complimenting	☐
Recommending rather than demanding	☐
Acceptance	☐
Collaboration	☐
Giving of yourself	☐
Respect	☐
Opportunities	☐
Growth	☐
Security	☐
Integrity	☐
Loyalty	☐
Inclusion	☐

Now that you've scored yourself for each individual, place the scores side by side. Are you consistent? Are you being very encouraging to one or more people (8's, 9's, and 10's) but not very encouraging to others (3's, 4's, and 5's)? If so, why the difference?

I seem to treat some of my people better than others because

_____

_____

Finally, how can you improve your own performance with your team as a whole and for specific individuals?

I can improve the way I encourage all my people by

_____

_____

I can improve the way I encourage [NAME] by _____

_____

I can improve the way I encourage [NAME] by _____

_____

I can improve the way I encourage [NAME] by _____

_____

I can improve the way I encourage [NAME] by _____

_____

I can improve the way I encourage [NAME] by _____

_____

I can improve the way I encourage [NAME] by _____

_____

WHICH BUSINESS
ARE YOU IN?

We are not in the coffee business serving people,
but in the people business serving coffee.

HOWARD SCHULTZ, FOUNDER, STARBUCKS

I purchased a two-loaf package of organic bread from Costco. After eating the first loaf (no, not in one sitting) I opened the second loaf and noticed it had begun to mold. Since the expiration date hadn't passed I took the moldy loaf back. At the returns desk I met a part-time clerk and requested an exchange for the one spoiled loaf. Since I had eaten the other loaf I just wanted to replace the remaining one. The young lady said, "No problem. Here is all your money back so you can buy a new two-pack." I said, "I know how this works. In three weeks the price of the two-pack will go up 80 cents so you can make up the money you lose on people like me. That's the food business. Please, you can just give me half my money back." To my surprise she responded, " We're not in the food business." I cocked my head to one side and asked, "What business are you in?" She responded, "We're in the membership business. We are in the business of obtaining and maintaining customers and then treating them so well they renew their memberships every year."

CHOOSING THE RIGHT BUSINESS

The message that Costco is, essentially, in the people business started with the CEO at headquarters in Washington State and has successfully made it's way down to approximately 700 stores. The message was received by this part-time employee who internalized it, identified with it, and made a decision based on a correct under-standing of Costco's business model. What do you think could have happened if Costco defined itself as being in the food business? I think you know. You've shopped at those places, and they think that if you don't buy their bread someone else will. Costco is clear about where they intend to leave their mark—with people, not food—and it makes them unique.

We've all heard the saying, "Is the glass half-full or half-empty?" The answer you choose reflects your perspective and how you understand the question. A person who answers, "The glass is half-full," is generally considered optimistic, a positive thinker. By looking at the glass as half-full she tends to think about how to fill the glass to the top. She is thinking about gains. Another person, who sees the glass as half-empty might focus on conserving the water she has left so as to avoid losses. How two people see the same problem in different ways has a lot to do with the solutions they create.

What if there was another way? What if the "half-full and half-empty" perspective is too limiting and actually keeps us from thinking creatively about the problem? What if a clever young girl, who has never heard the question before—and doesn't know how she's supposed to answer—looks at the glass and says this? "The glass is completely full." "Wait a minute!" her teacher asks. "What do you mean the glass is full?" Our clever young girl answers, "Well, it looks to me like it's half-full of water and half-full of air."

That's full to me.

CLARIFY YOUR BUSINESS

It's just like the three stonecutters I told you about before. One group of salon owners I work with believes they are in the hair business. The second group tells me how they see themselves as being in the service business. They say, "Sure we cut, color, and style hair but we're really in the service business." However, the most successful owners I work with are like the third stonecutter. They say,

| *"We're in the people business."*

This is what's important. As you think about leaving your mark, don't use your energy trying to change the hair and beauty industry and don't worry about "revolutionizing" the service business. Your true opportunity is to leave your mark with people—your clients and your team. Learn how to make people happy. Learn how to make them feel special. Learn how to lead them and support them.

Learn how to give them what they truly want and leave them better off than you found them. Learn to help them see how you and your salon are special. Do these things and your durable mark will be imprinted on them—not because of how you invested in them, or how you made them look, but how you made them feel about themselves and feel about you. If we all agree to do that, just one salon at a time, that's what will change the hair and beauty industry.

FROM BEHIND THE CHAIR

I often ask working stylists, "During a service, how much of your energy and emotion goes into the technical part? I mean, the cutting, coloring, and styling of your client's hair." Generally, what I hear back is, "Maybe, like 30% or so." In the beginning I was surprised at that answer but now I'm used to it. So, I ask, "Where does the other 70% go?"

Most of the stylists I've ever worked with—and I've worked with thousands—know on some level that they are in the people business. Why? Because when they answer my second question they often say,

> "The other 70% of my energy and emotion goes into listening and conversation, and into just being there for my clients. Sometimes I figure I must be the only person who simply let's them unburden themselves. For some reason they sure tell me a lot of stuff!"

The purpose of this chapter is to help you recognize, clarify, and proclaim what you, and most working stylists, already know.

| *You are in the people business.*

Remember that and make decisions based on it.

PEOPLE!

In the Introduction you read,

> **The purpose of this book** is to convince you that leaving your mark is the most important thing you will ever do. Each chapter is designed to help you achieve that by providing you with new thinking, people skills, and behaviors you'll need.

Helping you discover, define, and clarify your values, plus making you aware of the human need for significance, self-worth, and a sense of belonging is a strong foundation for your personal life and business life. Stimulating you to shift your thinking and recognize that it's not just about hair, it's not just about service—but it's really about people—is the strongest foundation I can give you for success in your business. So, what's the first thing we need to do in this people business? I'm glad you asked.

CREATE AN INDIVIDUAL EXPERIENCE

We already know that clients can walk into just about any salon and get a good/great color or cut. Technical skills and education are present throughout our industry. The important thing is what happens when the client leaves your salon. That's when the game begins to get interesting. Salons and stylists who create positive client feelings—and the education to help clients recreate their looks at home—win the game because their "hair high" doesn't just last a day, it lasts for weeks. By the way, to get a quick idea of how you're doing, look at your team's retention numbers.

> *People don't come in for a haircut. They come in for how the haircut makes them feel.*

We know that people skills differentiate top salons and stylists. In a study conducted by B. J. Gallagher, she found that 80% of people are failing in their current roles because they lack people skills. An informal survey in the beauty industry found that 85% of clients leave their current salon for non-technical reasons—in other words it's not because of the cut and color. It's because of how they felt after the cut and color.

In *The Wizard of Oz*, when the Scarecrow, Lion, and Tin Man ask the wizard for a heart, courage, and a brain the Wizard tells them, "You've had it all along." Just like the Wizard, your job as a stylist, with exceptional people skills, is to reveal qualities in your clients that are already there. With your technical training you've learned how to bring out the best in a client's physical traits—taking into account head shape, face shape, hair type, skin tone and color wheel, and so on. However, when it comes to using your people skills, are you connecting emotionally with your clients and boosting their significance, self-worth and sense of belonging? My friend Paul Vinod captured it very well when he observed, "People don't come in to have you color their hair as much as to color their thinking."

THE FIRST STEP

The first thing is to make every client feel special and to do it each and every time. It may be your ninth service of the day but remember it's her only time to feel beautiful for the next 3-6 weeks. Imagine the emotional reward if you make her feel like the only person in the world who matters for the next 60 minutes. Now imagine how let down she will feel if she realizes she's just another butt-in-your-chair during a crazy day of endless and random clients. Top stylists, with the highest retention, in our industry measure their success based on their ability to consistently create not only great looks but also stimulate an increase in significance, self-worth, and sense of belonging.

THE SECOND STEP

The next step is to listen. Focus on what's important to her as a person and not yourself as an owner or stylist. Tune in to her mood, her preferences, her communication style, and how she wants her appointment to flow. You wouldn't want to force an introvert to tell you her life story and you wouldn't expect an extrovert to be quiet for 60-90 minutes. Now, there are those clients who rely on you to "dish" or who live vicariously through you and want to hear about your weekend. Generally speaking, however, the last thing most clients want to talk about is you—and like most people—the first thing they want to talk about is themselves. This is supported by studies showing that the person who does the most talking usually feels better about how the conversation went than those who talked less. In other words, ask more questions, listen, and zip it!

THE FINAL STEP

The final step is to make an emotional connection with every client. The foundation of any good relationship is positive emotion. You may meet someone because you live in the same building, go to the same gym, or know someone in common. You become friends with her because you share common interests or share an activity. However, you become close friends when you connect emotionally. It works the same way with clients you want to retain for a lifetime. Every client wants to feel positive emotions as they think about coming to you, spending time in your chair, and as they anticipate their next visit. What is that emotion? That is your ultimate quest. For some it will be a feeling of significance. For some it will be to feel increased self-worth. For others it may be to experience a sense of belonging. (Are you starting to see how this works and how the more of this your clients experience the happier they are likely to be?) In any case, meet your clients where they are, and to the best of your ability, meet their emotional needs as you work your cutting, coloring, and styling magic.

OUR AMAZING ADVANTAGE

Many businesses say they want to make their clients feel special. The cool thing about our industry is that we have an unfair advantage. Hairdressing is one of the six professions where it is legal to touch the client. (Of course there are a few illegal ones too but I'll leave that to your imagination.)

Uncle Ben, in the movie *Spiderman*, says to Peter Parker "Remember, with great power comes great responsibility." The same is true for salon owners and stylists. What an amazing superpower and advantage we have:

Touch: Science shows how human touch stimulates the production of the hormone Oxytocin. The presence of Oxytocin in the brain is linked to very positive human emotions. This is the same chemical that is generated when a mother breastfeeds her child. In my work with a Psychologist in Atlanta I learned, "Make no mistake. Oxytocin is the chemical that bonds us as human beings." It increases trust, it reduces fear, and it even reduces the healing time for wounds. *Our opportunity for client intimacy is unmatched because we actually touch our clients in order to provide services.*

Frequency: From blowouts, to cuts & color, to the occasional up-do, women see their stylists anywhere from 6 to 50 times a year. That's huge! Did you see your best friend 50 times last year? How about your pastor? How about your doctor or your personal trainer? *Our opportunity to access our clients is unmatched because their hair refuses to stop growing and turning grey!*

Life Events: Engagements, weddings, births, christenings, first jobs, grandchildren, and even funerals. How many times have clients invited you to provide them services at these kinds of events? And, if they don't need your professional services they still invite you to attend as their guest. Except for moms and dads, a client's stylist may be present for more of her significant life events than any other person—let alone other professionals she only sees occasionally. (Can you even imagine inviting your lawyer to your wedding? Fuggitaboutit! Especially if they are responsible for the prenup.) *Our ability to develop durable relationships is ours if we choose it because very few women want to go through life without feeling good about their hair.*

BE UNIQUE

After speaking engagements it's pretty common for a salon owner to ask me to be Facebook friends. Never one to miss a teachable moment, I always ask, "How many friends do you have on Facebook?" Recently, a young lady answered, "3,346."

So here's my thing. I'm not interested in being anyone out of 3,346—and I don't want you to be either. If you are a salon owner, I want you to be unique. I want your salon and stylists to be unique. I want each of you to be better equipped to develop yourself and to share your vision! I want you to leave your mark—not get lost in the crowd. A recent study predicts that by 2018 we will have 757,700 stylists in the United States. Do you want your stylists to be just one of 757,700 or do you want them to stand out? As I travel around the country I can't escape the impression that most salons claim to be different but, if I'm being honest, they are all trying to be different in exactly the same way. This leads to a condition I call, "dynamically mediocre" where salon owners offer "an experience," by providing coffee, tea, and snacks, and they claim to offer "the best education in the industry."

As humans, we tend to want to be seen as different, but not too different. We want to be unique, but not weird. We want to be special, but still part of a group. However, when there are nearly 800,000 other stylists in the U.S. fitting in may just mean getting lost.

> *"You do not merely want to be considered just the best-of-the-best. You want to be considered the only one who does what you do."*
> -JERRY GARCIA

I'd like to ask you to take a few minutes right now and think about your team. Is each person seen as unique? Take another few minutes and challenge yourself. Is your salon truly unique, or offering the same things as other salons in your area?

SIGNATURE, SPECTACULAR, SUSTAINABLE

Apple, Coke, Disney. There are other computer, soft drink, and movie studios but these brands stand out because they create emotional connections with their customers. Apple makes customers feel smart and innovative and hip. Disney creates screen characters we really feel connected to. Coke sells us a couple minutes of happiness for $1.25 and free refills!

Great salons and stylists also understand they are a brand. Stan Slap shared an idea with me that I believe is one of the most immediate ways you can differentiate your brand. Make sure your brand is Signature, Spectacular, and Sustainable[1].

SIGNATURE

Merriam Webster defines signature,

> *Something (such as a quality or feature) that is closely associated with someone or something.*

Think of Nordstrom's handwritten "Thank you" note, Starbucks writing your name on your cup, or how the Southwest flight attendants will sometimes sing the inflight passenger announcement.

What do you do that makes you appear unique and that makes your clientele feel unique? Do you,

- Walk your clients to the front door and hug them when they leave?
- Help them with their coat and smocks?
- Send a hand written thank you note?
- Text them three days after their appointment asking how they are enjoying their cut or color?
- Stock their favorite tea?
- Give them a written consultation?

When you think of signature think of something different or unique. Don't settle for the common thing everyone does. For example, offering tea isn't signature but offering her favorite tea is. Offering a consultation isn't signature, but a written consultation that includes instructions for her in-home regimen is. Asking her how she likes her cut isn't signature but texting her three days later to see if she still likes it is.

What do you do that is "so you" that no one else is doing it? What do you do that is signature?

SPECTACULAR

Spectacular is simply what do you do that gets a "WOW!" from your clients. Wegmans Supermarket, always walks you to the item you are looking for. Ritz Carlton refers to you by name (even before you have given it to them). Zappos not only has a liberal returns policy but also empowers their customer service superstars to make customer satisfaction decisions on the spot. What do you do as a stylist that is spectacular? Do you,

- Offer a redo at no charge regardless of the time that has passed?

- Take product back for any reason at any time if they are not satisfied?
- Remember birthdays and anniversaries with a hand-written card?

As a salon owner you not only want your clients to feel your brand is spectacular, you want your team to feel the same way. One of the steps I've seen that make stylists feel spectacular is when owners do away with non-compete contracts and simply focus on creating a compelling vision that anyone would love to be part of and stay with for a lifetime. To borrow thinking from another industry, Gensler, an architecture and design firm, values the idea that employees who leave often "boomerang" back to them in the future. Employees, who leave, only to return, bring with them new experiences, know-how, and an appreciation for Gensler that improves their company. I know that ignoring non-competes disrupts conventional wisdom, and may even ruffle some feathers, but that's what great brands do. What do you do that is spectacular—and maybe a little disruptive?

SUSTAINABLE

In the beginning of a romantic relationship you may have received flowers, candy, and little love notes. This made you feel special because they were a nice surprise. However, as time went on they didn't sustain the same feelings for you. They were still a pleasure to receive but your significant other had to mix it up a little to keep the surprises coming and sustain your feelings. Doing the same thing over and over doesn't generate the same feeling over and over. Researchers, writing in a recent issue of *The Journal of Neuroscience*, say it appears the brain responds much more strongly to the unexpected than to the merely pleasurable. Research reveals a counterintuitive truth: our best memories are the surprising ones. We feel most comfortable when things are certain, but we feel most alive when they're not. Dr. Read

Montague, an associate professor of neuroscience at Baylor University believes, "…People are designed to crave the unexpected." Birchbox, a subscription service that sends customers a box of mystery beauty products each month and Phish, the rock band that never performs the same show twice, prove that entire business models can be built around this insight about unexpectedness.

If you do the same cut, using the same education, the same style, the same conversation, and the same consultation, you're going to go stale at some point. That's when you're vulnerable to losing your client. To sustain an emotional connection with your client you not only have to "send her flowers," you also have to come up with the occasional, "Lunch in Paris." What are you doing to upgrade your client experience from pleasurable to unexpected? The unexpected quickly becomes the pleasurable. Great salons embrace this little secret and continually provide the unexpected.

EXERCISE

What is signature, spectacular, and sustainable about you and your brand? This is a question you need to ask yourself at least once a month. Take ample time to fill in the blanks in the following exercise. If you work alone, come back to this exercise each month to renew your understanding and focus. If you own a salon, share your vision with your team and see if you can drive something signature, spectacular, and sustainable across your entire salon.

What is signature? _____

_____

What is spectacular? _____

_____

What is sustainable? _____

_____

I know from experience there is more to this simple exercise than meets the eye. We spend so much time focusing on our clients, our team, and managing our expenses that it can be tough to think deeply about our brand and how we differentiate ourselves. If you had trouble filling in the blanks, sleep on it. Come back to it in the morning with fresh eyes—and give it another try. Come back to this exercise again each month.

WITH GREAT POWER COMES GREAT RESPONSIBILITY

Your talent is God's gift to you.
What you do with it is your gift back to God.

LEO BUSCAGLIA

The Justice League, known around the world for members with superpowers, is looking for new superheroes. Somehow you've gotten into the interview process to work alongside Aquaman, Batman, and the Flash in fighting crime and promoting, well, justice all around the world. While you wait in the reception area for your turn to interview you see Superman and Green Lantern going into the office, just as Wonder Woman is coming out. You leap from your chair to ask her, "What are the questions like in the interview?" She responds "There is only one question: 'What is your superpower?'" You respond, "Superpower?" Wonder Woman replies, "Yes. What is your strength or gift?" She then wishes you good luck as she adjusts her weaponized tiara, checks her magical sword, and makes off to vanquish the nearest supervillain.

How do you think you'll do in the interview? How will you answer, "What is your superpower?" In my experience, most people would answer, "I don't know." Of course, that would immediately eliminate you from getting into the Justice League. More to the point, what other opportunities have you missed in your life because you did not know, embrace, or leverage your strengths? When you have strengths, but you don't recognize them, they're of no use to you or anyone else.

Superman was sent to Earth from Krypton. As a young child he started stumbling across his gifts. He lifted his crib above his head with one hand, hoisted a tractor off the ground, and he ran much faster than kids his age. Because his parents didn't understand his powers they suppressed them. Not that any of our parents ever suppressed us, but does this sound familiar? Superman's early years were awkward at best.

In high school his gifts continued to reveal themselves. In the beginning, he struggled because he didn't understand them and he couldn't control them. He flew into the side of his barn. He ran so fast he dug holes in the ground. Without an understanding of his gifts they were of no use. Once he was able to identify, explore, and embrace his strengths, things got better—*a lot better!* Soon he was faster than a speeding bullet. He leapt tall buildings in a single bound and he could stop a locomotive. As his confidence grew he went from being insecure and passive to confident and assertive. What others thought of him no longer defined him. He knew his gifts. He knew his purpose was to save people and save the world. He developed a sense of significance, self-worth, and sense of belonging. But what if Superman had never realized his gifts? The world would have missed out on one of its greatest citizens and would have been worse off because of it.

EVERYONE HAS A SUPERPOWER

Like every member of the Justice League, every one of us has a superpower. (For starters, we're all real people.) We may not have Wolverine's "healing factor," but each of us has strengths. Whether our strengths have to do with artistic vision, an ability to work with people, dexterity, being good with numbers, being good with words, an ability to speak in public, or to finish a book a week; we can all do at least one thing well.

WHAT'S AT STAKE?

> *The world is a better place when you identify, explore and embrace your special gift or superpower.*

For years, I had a successful career working in various industries including retail, consulting, and at a world-renowned hair care brand in New York City. Even though I was building a life and a career, somehow I still felt unfulfilled. In fact, I used to feel drained at the end of my workdays. Instead of being excited to go to work, it felt more like a duty—something I had to do but didn't want to do. I wasn't satisfied with my life but I couldn't quite figure out why. Then, after a long time exploring my feelings, thinking about it, and asking my friends and family for advice, someone said, "When you speak in public you seem like a different person. You're dynamic, funny, and you can take complex ideas and present them in ways anyone can understand." That was the insight I needed. That person gave me the gift of a lifetime. She brought into focus something I had been searching for unsuccessfully for years.

She helped me name my superpower.

Once I was able to name it I began to use my strengths to help me leave my mark. Just like Superman, I began to understand and develop my strengths rather than suppressing, misusing them, and running into the sides of barns. I put more of my time and energy behind doing the thing I was best at and spending less time doing things I would never be good at—or that didn't play to my strengths. In fact, I started to notice that whenever I work within my strengths it takes less energy. On the other hand, whenever I work on something where I'm not strong, it takes an enormous amount of energy to complete even the smallest task.

The benefits I experience are the same ones I want for you— because they will help you leave your mark.

BENEFITS OF KNOWING YOUR STRENGTHS

When you know your strengths it's like getting a booster shot from life. You are able to:

- Feel less insecure and passive
- Feel more secure, confident, and assertive
- Reduce undesirable emotions and behaviors like aggression, passive-aggressiveness, and anger
- Increase desirable emotions and behaviors that lead to significance, self-worth, and a sense of belonging.

WHAT IS YOUR SUPERPOWER?

You may already know your superpower. On the other hand, if you're like I was, it may not be clear to you yet. Unlike Sway, none of us has the ability to stop time—so the sooner you discover your strengths, the better. Here is an exercise I developed to help you move from where you are to where you need to be—and to do it in as little time as possible.

- Find three to five people who know you well (teacher, parent, sibling, spouse, boyfriend, girlfriend, pastor, coworker, manager, subordinate).
- Tell them you're not looking for compliments. Explain that you're taking an inventory and you would like to know what they see as your top three strengths. Ask them to think about what you do well.
- Their answers will give you several strengths that others see in you.
- Pay particiular attention to strengths that were repeated by more than one person.
- Of those, focus on one, two, or three strengths and explore whether they resonate with you.
- If they do, you now are very likely to know what your strengths or superpowers are. (Or at least ready to give them a test flight.)
- If your strengths take you to the next level, or help you be the best person you can possibly be, then you've hit the jackpot.
- You can now fulfill your purpose in life, and pass the Justice league interview, because you now know the answer to, "What is your strength or superpower?"

ACKNOWLEDGE YOUR WEAKNESSES, FOCUS ON YOUR STRENGTHS

You can't ignore your weaknesses but you shouldn't obsess over them either. It is so much easier, and more energizing when we work, play, and create in areas where we are strong. Performing in areas where we are weak is so much harder and it drains us.

Here are the practical reasons you want to spend as much time as possible in areas where you are strong.

STRENGTHS	WEAKNESSES
Give you confidence	Steal your confidence
Give you energy	Consumer your energy
Create time	Take your time
Lead to peak performance	Lead to under performance
Help you leave your mark	Help you leave a stain

As a separate exercise, identify and acknowledge your weaknesses. Rather than just ignoring them, or avoiding them, put together a plan to improve your weakness. Since everyone has limitations, there will be some areas where you will never excel—and that's going to be OK. The best any of us can do is to gravitate toward our strengths and improve our weaknesses as best we can.

Notice that a weakness may not be something you do poorly. It might actually be something you do well but requires way too much energy. For example, a weakness of mine is focusing on details. I learned to do it very well but I did it by overcompensating. I can focus on details like nobody's business but it takes so much energy for me to do it that I have to check into OCD rehab after every time I do it.

Here is some room to make your notes—I've provided one example of a common weakness to get your thinking started.

STRENGTHS	MY PLAN	MY GOAL
1. I shut down when I'm faced with new things.	To work on my listening skills so I don't assume the worst.	Stay open-minded for at least one day before rejecting something.
2.		
3.		
4.		
5.		

IMPLICATIONS FOR LEADERS

Identifying your superpower, using and developing them, and avoiding getting wrapped up in your weaknesses—as much as possible—applies as much to stylists as it does to salon owners, leaders, and managers. No matter what your role is, your superpower helps you leave your mark—not to mention helping others leave theirs.

Salon owners and managers, in particular, have a special opportunity to help their brands, their organizations, and themselves by assisting each member of their teams to discover their own strengths; and then put those strengths to work creating loyal clients. It is the responsibility of every salon owner, leader, and manager to take each individual's natural talent and develop it to its maximum potential.

Your job is to identify strengths in others specifically to:

- **Help** your people reach their own potential and leave their mark.
- **Assign** the right responsibilities to the right people so your clients benefit the most.
- Help your people **specialize** and standout. This is common, e.g., when one person specializes in three-dimensional color, another in weddings and updos, while another specializes in men's cuts, and so on.
- **Translate** your people's feeling of success into higher levels of performance —which leads to more business for them, and for you, because of happier and more loyal clients.

EXERCISE

Over the next fourteen days, carefully assess the strengths of your team. Do this by using the following table to help you organize your assessment of each employee. In fact, give a copy of this table to everyone and ask them to hand in their own self-assessment. Once you compare notes, take action to put the right people into the right jobs to create the right results for you and your clients. I've given you two examples to get you started.

Continue to exercise on the next page.

NAME	STRENGTHS	WEAKNESSES	COACHING			
Andrea	Cutting and coloring	She's very shy	Ask, "What could you do to start getting over being shy?"			
Joy	Very energetic & youthful	Dominates conversations	Ask, "What two things could you do to get clients talking more?"			

GOT TRUST?

*To be trusted is a greater compliment
than being loved.*

GEORGE MACDONALD

A few years ago I read Stephen Covey Jr.'s book, *The Speed of Trust*. For me, it was like putting on a new pair of glasses that gave me 20/20 vision. I was so taken with the message of the book I called the company and signed up for their workshop. I was so impressed by the workshop I took the certification course so I could bring Covey's message to you.

Here is what I now know to be true:

> *"Trust allows leaders to do things better, faster, and at lower cost[3]."*

TRUST—IT'S COMPLICATED

When we trust someone it's usually because we think they have our best interests at heart. We also tend to trust people who will do what they say, who have the knowledge and experience to do what we need, and who have a proven track record of results. Even then, however, who we trust, and what we trust them with, isn't always straightforward. Like the relationship status on Facebook that says, "It's complicated," trust is complicated. It doesn't just vary from person to person. It also varies from task to task. In the salon world this is why your clients may go to one stylist for cuts and to another for color. It may be why they go to one salon for their mani-pedis and another salon for their blowouts.

Trust isn't a yes-or-no thing. If I'm your client I may trust you to have my best interests at heart and to cut my hair to my liking. At the same time, I may not trust you to do my color if you didn't do a good job on me last time. So, depending on the situation, the nature of the problem, and what they need from us, our clients select the right person to trust. We trust different people for different things based on the situation and our needs from them at the time.

In our industry we talk a lot about trust, however, we disguise it by referring to a metric that we call *retention*. For example, if you have 68% retention then 68% of your clients *trust* you enough to rebook with you. Unfortunately, that also means 32% of your (former) clients didn't trust you enough so they left. I have always argued that, when you get right down to it, "retention" means "trust" and it is people's trust we are really measuring.

| *Retention = TRUST*

"Only 68% of your clients trust you," is a much clearer message than, "Your retention number is 68%." Not only does it place the focus where it should be, it let's us ask, "Did you lose them because of something in your character or something to do with your competence?" What would it take for you to focus on trust instead of retention? This shift in thinking will increase your referrals, rebookings, reviews, and retention—because retention=trust.

A PRECISE DEFINITION OF TRUST

Because there are several pieces that go into determining who trusts whom, understanding the nature of trust is easier if we break it down. That is why I promote the definition of trust that Stephen Covey Jr. uses in *The Speed of Trust*[3]. It makes things plain and simple.

| *"Trust = character + competence."*

In other words, if you trust someone it's because you trust their character and you trust their competence. If they trust you, it's for the same reason.

DEFINITION OF CHARACTER

Let's dive in a little deeper to understand what we mean by character.

Like trust, character is also made from two pieces.

> *"Character = intent + integrity[3]."*

INTENT

Intent is **why** you do something—or what motivates a particular behavior. Let's use an example to explain intent. In my experience, your stylists will generally say they do not like to sell retail products because they're not sales people. After hearing this claim a thousand times, I've come to believe the real reason stylists do not like selling retail is because they don't want to have their character questioned—especially their intent. Does this conversation sound familiar?

> STYLIST: Sara, as good as I am, I could not have achieved your look today without these products.
> CLIENT: Oh Tiffany, you're just trying to sell me product!

The way the client reacted makes it sound like she is questioning Tiffany's intent. She is suggesting that Tiffany is just trying to "sell" her rather than help her—even though Tiffany really meant it: *she could not have achieved the look without the right products.* There is no reason to believe that Tiffany had anything but pure intentions. She simply wanted to help her client duplicate her look at home. However, her client interpreted her words as "selling" and, therefore, she didn't trust her intentions. The best way to avoid this is to clarify your intentions from the beginning. Let's see how the conversation might look when we take this clarifying approach.

> STYLIST: Sara, how do you like your look today?
> CLIENT: It's perfect—as always! You know that.
> STYLIST: Thank you. What is your comfort level in creating this look at home?

CLIENT: Not very comfortable actually. I can never get these kinds of results.

STYLIST: Well, my intent is to help you get these results at home. I couldn't create your look without the products and tools I use. Would you like me to explain how to use them?

CLIENT: Yes. I think part of my problem is that I don't know what to use or how to use them.

Two people often experience the same thing, event, or conversation in completely different ways. When I do something, I judge myself by my intent because I know "why" I do things (most of the time) and my intent is clear to me. Even though I think what I'm trying to do or say should be obvious, no matter how hard I try, the other person just can't read my mind! So, they don't judge me by my intent—they judge me based on my actions. In our first example, Sara perceived Tiffany's words as an act of trying to sell her product—even though she got Tiffany's intentions all wrong.

In our second example, whether you use Tiffany's exact words or use your own, the key is to tip the outcome in your favor by expressly clarifying your intent before the other person is tempted to read your mind and probably misjudge you. Don't leave it to chance. Be mindful and start your statements with, "My intent in saying this is…" usually that is enough to prevent the other person from misunderstanding you and making wrong assumptions about your intent. Here are some examples to give you a feel for how stating your intent improves understanding by putting your true motives on the table.

MOTHER (typical): "You need to be home by 11:00 p.m."

CHILD: "I'm too old for a curfew."

MOTHER (restated with intent): "My intention is for you to be safe. Having you home by 11:00 p.m. allows me to get some rest knowing you are safe."

CHILD: "So, you're not trying to control me or treat me like a child."
MOTHER: "No, not at all. I just worry and then I can't sleep."

STYLIST (typical): "We don't have enough education."
OWNER: "I offer education and no one shows up."
STYLIST (restated with intent): "My intent is for our salon to be the best. More education and different types of education would help us improve."
OWNER: "I'm so glad you care enough to say something. What are your ideas?"

OWNER (typical): "You need to keep your work area clean."
STYLIST: "You are always on us about everything."
OWNER (restated with intent): "My intention is to create a space that is visually appealing for clients and employees. It's up to all of us, working as a team, to keep our work area and our common areas clean.
STYLIST: "I understand your intention. I want the same thing. If you book me on the 45 vs. 30 that will allow me to clean as I go."

INTEGRITY

Integrity is **doing what you say** you are going to do. You may be familiar with the saying, "Walk the walk—don't just talk the talk." Your stylists might say they will do many things—but what they actually follow through with is what you and others judge them by. Examples include:

- Starting on time
- Finishing on time
- Offering the newest cuts
- Making hair healthier

- Offering the best in hair care products and tools
- Performing a consultation each and every time
- Making clients feel better and look better.

The question is, do they follow through? Do they "Walk the walk"?

When we don't deliver on our promises we impact our integrity and damage our character. This damage then diminishes our clients' trust. If our clients don't trust us they will not rebook, let alone refer us, or give us good reviews online.

DEFINITION OF COMPETENCE

Like trust and character, our definition of competence is made up of two parts:

> *"Competence = capabilities + results[3]."*

CAPABILITIES

Capabilities are **can you do it?** Technical education plays such a strong role in our industry because it helps determine our capabilities. It increases the number of things we can do. Our trainings, titles, certifications, and portfolios symbolize our capabilities. If you ask many salon owners and stylists they will tell you, "Education is the most important part of our culture." What they are saying is that they are capable—and, "The more capable we are, the more competent we are. The more competent we are, the more you can trust us."

Let's use the example of going to the doctor. Prominently displayed on every physician's wall is a copy of his or her diploma. Why? It's because doctors want to earn our trust very quickly. Diplomas are powerful symbols of capabilities. The diploma came from a school, and certain schools are able to charge more than others. Why? Because we trust some schools more than other schools to graduate capable doctors. That creates a higher demand for doctors from those schools. Let's say you're considering two doctors. One has a diploma from Harvard and the other received his diploma online. Which doctor do you immediately trust more?

It works exactly the same way in our industry. Some salons and stylists charge more because they are able to generate more trust based on their capabilities. So, borrow a lesson from the medical profession and prominently display and talk about your certificates, diplomas, and awards for your technical and client service skills. It's a simple and effective way to let the world know, "I am capable!"

This is how we operate knowingly and unknowingly as human beings. We are drawn to, shop from, socialize with, and date people we trust. This is the most compelling reason to invest in your technical education and then hang your license, certifications, and diploma on your wall. You do it to build your clients' trust in your capabilities.

When clients trust your capabilities it gives you advantages as a salon, a brand, or as an individual stylist. One example is your ability to charge more for your services. Think about the last time your newest stylist raised her prices. Was she afraid to tell her clients personally? Did she skip the conversation altogether—or leave it to the front desk to notify them? Why? Maybe she didn't have her clients' trust. Did you step in to coach her and explain that it would be easy to have this kind of conversation if she had already earned her clients' trust? When we have our clients' trust we can smile and say with confidence, "I am excited to share with you that based on my education and experience I have received a promotion and will be moving to the next level next month! With that move my prices will be moving to $60. I am excited and wanted you to be one of the first to know."

RESULTS

Results answer the question, "**What has actually been done?**" Results are what happen when you follow through on delivering something you're capable of. If you say you can create a graduated bob you are talking about your capabilities. When you deliver a graduated bob for a client with the right head shape, face shape, and fashion sense—then you are creating results. If you say you are capable of cutting men's hair but most guys don't come back for a second appointment, it's probably because you are not delivering results.

IT AIN'T EASY!

I urge you to read—and reread—this chapter until you can recite the following from memory:

- Trust = character + competence
- Character = intent + integrity
- Competence = capabilities + results.

Post these three definitions in your break room and reread them until you understand them. When these ideas become second nature, anyone in your salon will be able to figure out which clients trust you—which ones don't—and then decide what to do about it.

To make things a little more real, it's important to understand each piece that goes into building trust has to be constantly considered in relation to all the other pieces. For example, a client may trust your intent, integrity, and your capabilities but still not rebook. Why? Let's say they trust your desire to please them (intent) and that you really did attend the education and earn your certification (integrity) and that you know how to perform a particular service (capability) but what you delivered simply didn't look good on them (results).

For complete trust to exist it must satisfy: intent + integrity + capabilities + results; **all at the same time.**

THE TRUST GAP

In my discussions with salon owners and stylists they often ask me, "Is it easier to recover from a breach of trust in character or in competence? I explain that it's always easier to recover from a breach in competence. Let me explain with an example right out of our national news. Target Corporation had a data breach in 2014 that affected the credit card information of about 110 million of its customers. The breach of trust cost them hundreds of millions of dollars. When hackers hit Target and exposed their customers' credit card information it caused their customers to mistrust Target's competence. How many of you, like me, still shop at Target today? My guess is that most of us still shop there. Why? Their failing was related to competence because the results didn't keep their customers' data secure (competence = capabilities + results). We all make mistakes and, as long as we know the other person is doing their level best, we tend to give them a second chance to get better results next time. Let's compare that to another kind of trust we saw play out in the national news.

Enron was an American energy, commodities, and services company back in the 1990's. Before its bankruptcy in 2001 Enron employed approximately 20,000 people and was one of the world's major electricity, natural gas, communications, and paper companies. It had revenues as high as $111 billion and Fortune Magazine named Enron "America's Most Innovative Company" for six consecutive years. However, behind that supposed innovation, was a culture of accounting fraud that misled investors about Enron's financial strength. Fraud is lying. Lying is a breach of character and bad intent. Enron is no longer in business—not because they weren't good at lying and cheating—they were really good at it. They lost the confidence of their customers, regulators, and investors because their intentions were bad. When customers don't trust your intent, they leave (character = intent + integrity).

That's why it's easier to recover from a breach of competence (Target) than from a breach of character (Enron).

In our industry an informal study in 2015 asked this question of clients, "What makes you leave a salon?" 85% said they left because of non-technical reasons. In other words it wasn't because of competence. They left because of issues where something didn't add up with the salon's or the stylist's character (intent + integrity).

TRUSTING A WHOLE PERSON

At the beginning of this chapter I mentioned that trusting someone isn't always a yes-or-no thing. Trust depends on the role a person plays at a given time. For example, an owner may trust a stylist with three-dimensional color but not with cutting and styling. She may trust her to have the salon's back while, at the same time, not trusting her to become an educator. It works the other way around too. A stylist may trust the salon owner as a working stylist but not trust her as a mentor. She may trust her people skills but not trust her financial skills.

Understanding this phenomenon is a very useful tool when you set out to build trust in other people—or earn the trust of others. Rather than saying, "I trust her" or, "I don't trust her," find one aspect of the other person you trust and build on that. If you suspect you have not earned someone's complete trust, break it down based on the definitions of character and competence. Here are three illustrations to show you what I mean.

STYLIST TO OWNER

A stylist wanted more new walk-ins than she was getting. Unknown to her the owner did not trust her with new clients. The stylist met with the owner to discuss her desires and began by pointing to her years of education, experience, and certifications. In our terminology, the stylist emphasized her competence. As it turns out, her competence was not an issue for the salon owner. For whatever reason, the owner didn't trust the stylist's character. Do you see the issue? The stylist assumed she wasn't getting her fair share of the walk-ins because of her perceived competence but the salon owner was on an entirely different page and couldn't hear the stylist's argument because she was hung up on the stylist's character.

The opportunity, for salon owners and stylists alike, is to simply ask the other person, "Where would you like to have a greater level of trust with me?" That way you don't have to guess. Once you hear the answer you can translate that into *Trust = character + competence* and start to pinpoint the area for improvement. If the owner has concerns with a stylist's ability to hold appropriate conversations and come to work on schedule, you can imagine how emphasizing one's years of education, experience, and certifications would be a waste of time.

OWNER TO STYLIST

An owner I know in Boston wanted his team to include a written consultation in every client experience (sound familiar?). However, his stylists were hardly following through with written consultations at all. The reason his stylists were not complying was because they believed the written consultations were motivated by the salon owner's desire to sell more product and to make more money for himself. In other words, the stylists did not trust the owner's intent because they thought he was saying one thing but really meant another.

As it turns out, the owner had just returned from a workshop where the written consultation was described as an important part of a "brandable client experience." The consultants made a compelling argument that excellent salons differentiate themselves from mediocre salons when they include written consultations for their clients. After failing to get the consultations implemented, the owner decided to clarify his intentions as a way to overcome the mistrust of his stylists. He told his stylists that his intent was not to sell more products but to differentiate the salon. To back up his intentions, he removed the requirement for selling retail. "We will not have retail selling classes. It will not be part of your review. It will not be criteria for advancing from one level to the next. And, there will be no contests," he told them. Every stylist, as long as they were an employee in good standing, and supported the brand, culture, and its mission, would receive their monthly average retail commission, based on the prior year's sales, regardless of the amount they sold this year. The stylists were initially shocked into silence but quickly erupted into applause. They felt relief because they now understood the owner's intent and trusted how he backed it up by making money a non-issue.

After 24 months the salon was averaging 922 written consultations per month—which translated into an increase of 56% in sales, growing from $75,000 to $117,000. Because the owner was able to identify the area in which they needed to build trust (intent) they were able to make an adjustment that built trust to the point where they got the desired result and created a brandable experience for the salon and the stylists.

SALON TO CLIENT

I was working with a newly opened salon in New Jersey that offered free haircuts to new clients as a way to create new business. After a month, not one free-haircut had been redeemed. The owner said to me, "New clients don't trust my salon yet. They're not willing to let a such a new salon cut their hair." Because she figured out that new clients didn't trust her salon's capabilities, she modified her offer to something different that potential clients might trust.

She changed her promotion to free blowouts. Guess what? Clients who were not willing to trust her salon to cut their hair were actually willing to trust her salon to style their hair. She redeemed 35 free blowouts a week for eight straight weeks. She retained 93% of those new clients, booking them for a follow up cut. She successfully leveraged the small amount of trust they placed in her **capability** to do a blowout into a much larger amount of trust based on **results**; which then translated into successfully cross-selling clients from blowouts to full service!

ALL-CALL TO ACTION!

I am lucky to work with salon owners and stylists every day. After observing thousands of salon/stylist/client interactions, I've recognized many patterns of behavior that either increase or destroy trust and I've broken them down to make each one very clear and easy to understand. If you are like most salon owners and stylists I've met, there's probably something thought provoking for you here.

Continue to exercise on the next page.

AUDIENCE	CHARACTER		COMPETENCE	
	INTENT	**INTEGRITY**	**CAPABILITIES**	**RESULTS**
Clients	I will clarify my intent first, e.g., "My intention by recommending you rebook within 4 weeks is so your roots won't show."	I will be on time for my clients.	I will let clients know every time I complete ongoing education.	I will do a post-service consultation to better understand client satisfaction.
	"My intent behind recommending these products is so that you can duplicate this look at home."	I will clarify the costs of services as part of my consultation before I begin.	I will share my certifications and diplomas with my clients.	I will show my results in a portfolio or on a website, Facebook, or Instagram.
Peers	My intent is to build a better working relationship.	I will talk to you directly if I have an issue with you.	I will be open, honest, and on time with issues that come up between us.	I will be respectful and non-judgmental of you when we disagree & always be professional in our communication.
	My intent is to be part of a team that is known for great education.	I will go for education no less than twice a year.	I will share back with the team what I have learned in the form of a workshop.	You will have a high trust level in my skills, knowledge and ability.

AUDIENCE	CHARACTER		COMPETENCE	
	INTENT	INTEGRITY	CAPABILITIES	RESULTS
Peers	My intent is to be part of a fashion forward salon.	I will look in the mirror everyday to make sure I am living up to our salon standard.	I will research media to get ideas on what fashion is.	I will look and act the part of a professional in the beauty industry.
	My intent is to help the salon operate as a team.	I will be open to feedback on how I am as a team player.	I am willing to adjust my behavior based on the feedback of others.	I will participate in all meetings and focus on the solution not the problem.
Salon Owner	My intent is to make more money.	I will find a mentor and create a plan.	Where I am not strong I will ask for help.	I will hand out my card, ask for referrals, and offer to rebook all clients.
	My intent is to get more walk ins.	I will come in and stay late regardless of whether I have appointments.	I will continue to develop my people skills so that I am more of a match for different personality types.	I will retain more of my clients.

| AUDIENCE | CHARACTER | | COMPETENCE | |
	INTENT	INTEGRITY	CAPABILITIES	RESULTS
Myself	My intent is to be constantly learning.	I will go for education once a quarter.	I will post my certificates in a place that will create conversations with my clients.	At the end of the year I will have gone to no fewer than 4 classes for both technical and non-technical skills.
	My intent is to be a positive force in the salon.	I will not bring up a problem without a solution.	I will research solutions to outstanding issues.	I will be known as the person to go to for a solution.
	My intent is to show I am reliable.	If I will be late I will call ahead of time.	I will be 15 minutes early for my shift.	I will not be late.

EXERCISE

Now you try it. With the above tables in mind, think through the following questions and create your own answers.

What is your retention percentage? _____ %

What do you need to do to building up trust with your clients?

_____

_____

_____

What do you need to do to build up trust with your peers?

_____

_____

_____

What do you need to do to build up trust with your owner?

_____

_____

_____

What do you need to do to build up trust in yourself?

_____

_____

_____

AUDIENCE	CHARACTER		COMPETENCE	
	INTENT	INTEGRITY	CAPABILITIES	RESULTS
Clients				
Peers				
Salon Owner				
Myself				

EQ: GENIUS HAS
ITS LIMITS

*People with average IQs outperform those
with the highest IQs 70% of the time.*

TRAVIS BRADBERRY

I took the High School Equivalency Test, and then enrolled in a nearby junior college, mostly so I wouldn't have to take the Scholastic Aptitude Test (SAT) required by four-year colleges. I was intimidated by the SAT because I thought it would limit my future success. Rather than continuing to learn, explore, overcome obstacles, and reach my own God-given potential, I was afraid the test results would determine, not only my college experience, my job prospects, and my income, but also how successful and happy I would be for the rest of my life. For me, the only thing worse than having my fate determined by some test at the age of 16 would be to learn the day I was going to die—which I didn't want either. Yikes!

Society seemed to be telling me that success came from tests, studies, and college. Because my heart wasn't into school, what I needed was someone who could show me a path to success using my natural strengths and ignoring my weaknesses. Fortunately, my best friend's dad became that role model. Knowing his story literally opened doors in my mind and let me see my own potential. He barely finished high school and yet managed to make his fortune, lose it all, earn it all back again—and then some. He was willing to take risks, work hard, keep at it, and learn how to work with people and get the most out of his relationships. I was experiencing a certain amount of success by 16 and meeting him showed me that, in real life, there was a way forward for me.

With new hope and inspiration I graduated high school early. I found a job where I got along very well with people and I was put in charge. I had a strong social life and I was accepted as one of "the guys" on our basketball team. People often told me, "You're great to talk to. You are a good listener. You get me. You seem to know what I'm thinking. Let's hang out!"

If you are book smart, celebrate it because that is a wonderful God-given gift. On the other hand, if you're like me, and your path to success is based on a different kind of intelligence—a kind anyone can harness regardless of his or her own particular strengths and weaknesses—then this chapter is for you.

WHAT DETERMINES OUR FATE?

For years, successful stylists have told me how their jobs are partly hairdressing and partly knowing how to work with people. When I ask, "What part of your success on the job is due to technical skills and how much is due to people skills?" almost everyone answers:

- 60-90% of my job success comes from my people skills
- 10%-40% is from my technical hairdressing skills.

My follow up question is, "What percent of your education was technical and what percentage had to do with developing people skills?" Of course, you know the answer. Salon owners and stylists are trained almost entirely on technical skills, which are not the most important things for our long-term success. As an industry we place a high value on technical knowledge, education, and training and we place almost no value on learning the people skills that all successful business people possess. You earned your license by demonstrating purely technical competence. You kept your job by demonstrating technical mastery. You create a career, and leave your mark, by mastering your people skills.

I want you to leave your mark personally and professionally. That's why I ask you, "How much of your salon's educational calendar do you devote to helping your team learn how to make people feel good about themselves?"

You may ask, "What does this have to do with leaving my mark?" Well, like one of my favorite quotes from Maya Angelou reminds us,

People will forget what you said. People will forget what you did. But people will never forget how you made them feel.

WHAT IS IQ?

I imagine that most of us have at least some idea about what IQ (intelligence quotient) tests are, even if we haven't taken one. They are the tests that supposedly tell us how smart we are. In fact, they kind of tell us how smart we were born to be—and how smart we will always be—regardless of what we learn or accomplish in life. Once we're assigned our number (let's say 105) then that's our number forever.

WHAT IS EQ?

Recent research done since the 1990's recognizes a different kind of smarts. Emotional intelligence is a form of social intelligence. It's the ability to identify an emotion in yourself, and others, and then adjust your behavior based on that emotion. People who have it are more tuned into their feelings and the feelings of those around them. People with high EQs (emotional quotients) know how to perceive, use, understand, and manage their emotions to connect with others. And the beauty of emotional intelligence is that it can increase throughout our lives with no limit to how high our EQs can grow.

Think about your salon. Hairdressing is about:
- Hair (outside the head)
- External beauty
- Technical skills (cutting, coloring, and styling)
- IQ intelligence.

Think about your work with people. People skills are about:
- Brain (inside the head)
- Internal Beauty
- Non-technical skills (feelings, emotion, and relationships)
- EQ intelligence.

| *Our opportunity is to build our EQ.*

HOW IMPORTANT IS EQ?

My first job in the beauty industry was as a Sales Consultant with a company that is still one of the top hair care brands in the world. Seriously, they're so famous that you couldn't complete the sentence, "Bumble and _____," without guessing who they are. Now, since I am bald, I had no first-hand knowledge of hair care products or how to use them. That, along with no industry experience, made me someone with little experience and technical knowledge. At the time, I thought of myself as having a kind of "low IQ" in our industry. My first business trip was attending an eight-week training course in New York City along with all of our 33 Sales Consultants nationwide. On the fourth day we took a product knowledge test that covered 85 different products. The test was scored immediately and they gave us our results right away. At lunch, my regional manager and her Director asked if they could meet with me privately. After less than a week on the job I assumed I had exceeded their expectations and they wanted to congratulate me. (Yes, I tend to be blindly optimistic.) They started the conversation by telling me I scored a 65 on the product knowledge test. My response was, "That's GREAT!" How great? Well, unfortunately, they told me 65 was the lowest score they had ever seen. Oh great! They were pretty direct in telling me that my low score would make it very hard for me to succeed at the company. I was furious. What I had learned earlier in my career, and what I knew to be true, was that my EQ would determine my success not my IQ. I vowed, then and there, to prove myself on my own terms using my own strengths. The result? I finished that year as one of the top three Sales Consultants and I was recognized across the company for my outstanding performance. Not only did I feel vindicated and proud, I also earned a bonus of twice my base salary.

I'm not the only one who has benefited financially by trusting my EQ and developing it every chance I get. Several studies[4] have shown how people with high EQs are more successful.

- People with high EQs earn $29,000 more per year on average than their counterparts.
- 58% of job success is directly related to EQ (not IQ).
- 90% of top performers have higher EQs than their peers.

This means that your success has more to do with your people skills than your technical skills. What's more, you see it around you and in your own salon. Think about the stylist whose cutting and coloring is as good as you've ever seen, but she doesn't have a full book because she can't connect with people or figure out how to get along in the salon. Now think of the stylist whose cutting and coloring skills are average, yet she is fully-booked because her clients, you, and everyone else loves her. In fact, a salon owner in Arizona shared a story with me about when he was first starting out as a new stylist. A client told him, "You're not very good at cutting hair yet but I like you. I'll give six more tries."

The good news is this: To succeed, yes, you have to be proficient—good or even great—with hair. However, the success you are really looking for will come from your people skills. And, in that way we're lucky because our EQs, and our potential, are open to limitless growth throughout our lifetimes.

THREE STEPS TO DEVELOP YOUR EQ

There are many books just about developing your people skills. Based on my years of working with salon owners and stylists, I can summarize the essentials for you in just one chapter. So, if I could waive a magic wand above your head, here are the three people skills that every salon owner would master and then teach her stylists—starting tomorrow.

MAGIC SKILL #1: STOP TALKING

My wife and I were coming back from a social event. She noticed how a couple we met loved talking to me and what a great conversation they had. I said, "Really? I felt like they took advantage of my generosity to listen. I didn't get to say five words." Up to that night I had always known that leaving my mark was about taking action and making things happen. But after reflecting on that conversation, I realized that I could also leave my mark by not doing something. In this case, it was to stop talking and start listening.

You've been in social situations your entire life. Who do you think enjoys a conversation more, the person who talks the most or the person who talks the least? Say you meet someone at a party, a coffee shop, or at a church event and that person launches in and does all the talking. How does that make you feel? If the other person does all the talking, if they don't show an interest in you, and if they dominate and don't allow you to get a word in edgewise, I'm guessing the conversation went well for them but, for you, not so much.

Often in my workshops, stylists share how great their conversations go with their clients. Now, honestly, I have to admit this leads me to believe that those stylists are doing most of the talking. Who should be doing all the talking and how do you get that to happen?

> *You stop talking and you start asking questions.*

Once I lay this out, my workshops start to get interesting. Most of the time, someone will say, "How can I listen to them when my clients are always asking me, 'How are you doing?' 'How are your kids?' and 'What's new with you?'" What I tell my students is that people often ask those questions as a social courtesy—part of the way they demonstrate their social intelligence. However, *they may or may not* be truly interested in your answer. What they may really want is someone to listen to their story.

There is a skill to determining who is really interested, and who is practicing a social courtesy. The next time someone asks, "How are your kids?" reflect their question with, "They are doing great, but please tell me how your little one is doing." In my experience, 90% of the time they will take it from there. When that happens, you have succeeded. You stopped talking and started listening. On the other hand, if they come back to you with, "I know your daughter started soccer. How's that going?" you'll know they are actually interested in your answer and they're not just being polite.

The key to mastering this skill is to first reflect the other person's question by answering it with a question of your own. If their second question comes right away, they are telling you they are actually interested in hearing your story. If it never comes, you're giving them what they want—a chance to unburden themselves.

In my years of experience in salons, and in my personal life, rarely do I hear someone ask anyone that second question. Usually the first question functions kind of like a "Wazup?" In other words, it's like saying, "Hi." They're not really listening for a real answer. And you know what? I have to admit that used to kind of bug me. What has changed for me is the number of people who say they enjoy talking to me. Even though I remind myself that I'm in the business of helping others leave their marks, we're all in the business of making people feel good—and listening to people makes them feel good! So, that's why I do it—and you should too.

EXERCISE

Here are three practical conversations. Read the first three and then develop three of your own based on examples drawn from actual conversations you've had with your clients. (Hint: Can you spot the mistake the stylist makes in the first example?) Plan out your own unique replies to questions your clients ask you. Your replies should be questions that will help you determine if your clients are truly interested in you or if they are just being social and really came in for the chance to talk. Practice this until it is natural for you to reflect your client's questions and to give them what they really want.

A STYLIST WHO WANTS TO TALK

- **CLIENT**: "What did you do on vacation?"
- **STYLIST**: "We had a fantastic time. First, we flew down to Florida and then boarded our cruise ship. Let me tell you it was amazing…"

A STYLIST WHOSE CLIENT WANTS TO TALK

- **CLIENT**: "What did you do on vacation?"
- **STYLIST (reflecting the question)**: "We mostly lay on the beach and enjoyed adult beverages." "What are your vacation plans this year?"
- **CLIENT**: "Well, we're planning a road trip to collect souvenir spoons from all 50 states. We're starting in Florida and then…"

A STYLIST WHOSE CLIENT WANTS TO LISTEN

- **CLIENT**: "What are you doing this weekend?"
- **STYLIST (reflecting the question)**: "This weekend? It's all work and no play for me. What about you?"
- **CLIENT (showing genuine interest)**: "Come on Lindsay, dish. You know I never go out. Let me live a little! What are you doing? I'll bet it's fun."

• STYLIST (starting a dialog): "OK. I'll tell you but only because you sound like you're really interested—but then you have to promise to tell me your plans too. OK. So, Sam's picking me up at 8:00 p.m. on Saturday and…"

Now it's your turn. Remember, think about real conversations you and your team have recently had. What were these real examples like and how can you plan them out so they go better next time?

1. CLIENT: "_____."

2. STYLIST: "_____."

3. CLIENT: "_____."

1. CLIENT: "_____."

2. STYLIST: "_____."

3. CLIENT: "_____."

1. CLIENT: "_____."

2. STYLIST: "_____."

3. CLIENT: "_____."

MAGIC SKILL #2: ACKNOWLEDGE AND QUESTION INSTEAD OF DEFEND AND EXPLAIN

The second skill I would use my magic wand to instill in every stylist is the ability to acknowledge and question rather than defend and explain. Any time we are challenged, it is human nature to defend and explain our position.

For example, if a client tells us our products are too expensive, it's normal to react by defending and explaining all the features and benefits of our products. This triggers the client to defend and explain how she can get the same products cheaper at the drug store or on the internet. She doesn't hear the features and benefits information you told her about because she's already doubled-down on her defend and explain reaction, supporting her position with more blah, blah, blah.

Another common example is when a client tells us our services are too expensive. We react with "defend and explain" by saying something lame about how everything is going up including eggs, gasoline, and rent. Then the client defends and explains how her old stylist never raised her prices (whether that's true or not). She doesn't hear the information about how everything is going up in price because, again, she's loading up with her counter argument before you're even finished talking.

Stop me if you've heard this one; a salon owner raises her voice to that one stylist who just can't quite seem to get her act together, "You're late." The stylist immediately defends and explains how bad the traffic was, or how her kids are sick, or how her dog threw up on the neighbor's carpet. The salon owner takes the bait only to defend and explain how she has a business to run and being late isn't going to cut it. Neither party hears what the other person is really saying because both are dug deeply into their positions.

I'm sure you're starting to recognize this defend and explain behavior. You know what? It doesn't have to be this way. You can hear the other person—and the other person can hear you in return. The first step is to stop defending and explaining. The second step is to use an alternative approach that works much better because it takes advantage of the way our human brains are wired.

There is a neuron in our brain that acts like a mirror. Because of this mirror neuron, when you defend and explain your position, I will almost automatically defend and explain my position. Instead of the other person attacking us, and then having to defend ourselves, what we all want is for the other person to acknowledge our feelings and experiences. What we need to learn to do is called, *acknowledge and question* instead of defending and explaining.

> | *Stop defending and explaining.*

> | *Start acknowledging and questioning.*

Acknowledging is simply letting the other person know "I get you." You do this by saying something like, "You seem frustrated, (or upset) (or angry)." The skill is in hearing the other person and then using your best guess to name what they could be feeling or experiencing. By naming the feeling, the other person perceives that you are listening and that you're trying to relate to his or her experience.

Defending and explaining leads to tit-for-tat responses that often escalate into disagreements. On the other hand, when we acknowledge the other person, a chemical called serotonin is released in the brain that causes us to relax. It takes us out of our volatile emotional place and allows us to think more calmly and rationally. By acknowledging the other person you are laying the groundwork to ask questions to help you better understand the other person's situation, beliefs, or emotions. Once you do that, notice how the conversation changes.

Read these dialogues to see how possibilities emerge. Acknowledge the other person and then ask a question.

- • CLIENT: "Your products are too expensive."
- • STYLIST (acknowledges and questions): "It sounds like price plays a role in determining which products you purchase. What is the most important thing to you when you buy products?"
- • CLIENT (exposes her true feelings): "Well, what's most important to me is performance."
- • STYLIST: "Product performance is important to me too. That's why I used these products. What's your perception of the performance of these products today on a scale of 1-10?"

The moral of this story is that we're already on a better path. Even if she doesn't buy from you the conversation will be constructive and real. The conversation focuses on what's truly important and gives you insights you didn't have about your client. Those insights might not sell her a product today but they may help you retain a client for life.

- **CLIENT**: "Your services are too expensive."
- **STYLIST (acknowledges and questions)**: "You're not the first person to share that with me. What were you planning to spend and what did you want to have done?"
- **CLIENT**: "I was planning to get a cut and color within my budget of $120.00."
- **STYLIST**: A cut and color today would be $140.00. If you need to come in under $120.00, what I could suggest is that we do the more important service for you today and reschedule the other service for next week. Which is more important to you today, your cut or your color?"
- **CLIENT**: "That doesn't help me. I still need to stick to $120.00"
- **STYLIST**: "I totally get that. Here's what we can do. My coworker Michele has great education and experience and I've seen her do some amazing work. Her prices would allow you to get the cut and color you want for $120.00. I would be delighted to introduce her to you."

- **OWNER**: "You're late!"
- **STYLIST (acknowledges and questions)**: "I realize I wasn't here on time. Is there something urgent or time sensitive?"
- **OWNER**: "Of course there is something time sensitive your client arrived 15 minutes early and now she's been here for 30 minutes!"
- **STYLIST**: "Again, I acknowledge that I was late and now I know it's impacting my client. Do you want me to handle this or would

you like to say something to her?"

• **OWNER**: "No. You take care of it. But, please let me know if this situation is going to hurt our chances to rebook her."

MAGIC SKILL #3: DON'T JUDGE

Do you have clients who drain you, bring out the worst in you, and cause you to say things you don't mean? You know the type. They're always late. They word-vomit, and everything they say seems negative. They drain your energy. They tip poorly or not all. They won't pre-book. They never refer you. In fact, these are the clients you don't even call by name; you call them your "3:30," or your "4 o'clock."

My business partner once said to me, "If we only did business with people we liked, we wouldn't be in business," and I'm sure that's true for you too. As I visit salons I really keep that in mind. I've noticed the best salon owners and top-performing stylists know how to handle tough clients. Their secret is,

> *They don't judge.*

The owners and stylists with the highest EQs choose to believe that there is at least one good thing in each and every client. They believe if they look for something positive they will find it. Alpine skiing instructors teach, "Where you look is where you go." The same is true for your thinking. There is ample evidence that our brains will subconsciously find data to support whatever we believe is true. If you think a person is an idiot, I promise you will find all kinds of evidence to support your belief. But, if you believe a person has a good trait, your brain will find data to support your belief. Let me give you an example.

The client you dread, the one you refer to as your "3:30," walks into your salon. You've decided to believe the good Lord put at least one positive trait in every person. Knowing that, you start looking for it. You notice through the front window that she drove up in a nice car. The first comment you make is, "I love your car." She says, "Yes! Thank you! It's my first car. When I picked it up it was the best day of my life." Then she goes on to say, "You see, I was raised by a single mom who would get me up every morning to catch a bus together. Everyday when we passed this one car dealership she put her hand on my knee and said 'All I want for you baby is for you to have your own car.' The first thing I did after signing the paperwork for my car was to drive over to my mom's apartment and take her to dinner. On the way to dinner, we passed that same car dealership and my mom began to cry. She said, 'This is the best day of my life. When I used to tell you I wanted you to have your own car, what I was really saying was that I wanted you to have a better life than I could provide. Today my dream came true'."

Now, do you feel different about this client? Who changed? (You did!) What changed? (Your thinking!) Her behavior didn't change but your perception of her changed based on your openness to the good inside her. People with high EQs have the ability to recognize emotions in themselves, and in others, and adjust their own thinking, feelings, behaviors, and actions. Simply being able to recognize that you are not fond of a client is the first step in removing judgment. The next step is to begin looking for the one good thing in every client that can shift your thinking.

Your **thinking** drives how you **feel**[6].

Your feelings drive your **behavior.**

Your behavior drives your **actions.**

Shift your thinking and the rest will follow on the way to leaving your mark.

EXERCISE:

Think of three clients that you:

- Don't look forward to seeing
- Spend only enough time to get them out of your chair
- Would gladly hand off to another stylist.

For each of these clients, think of one positive thing that you will look for during their next appointment.

NAME:

What I used to focus on was my dislike for her _____

_____.

The positive thing I will look for relates to her _____

_____.

NAME:

What I used to focus on was my dislike for her _____

_____.

The positive thing I will look for relates to her _____

_____.

NAME:

What I used to focus on was my dislike for her _____

_____.

The positive thing I will look for relates to her _____

_____.

GET UP! GET ON UP! GET UP OFF OF THAT COUCH!

Life begins at the end of your comfort zone.

NEALE DONALD WALSH

Each year, across the country, thousands of people are brave enough to share their fears with me. Mostly, people are afraid of being uncomfortable. They are afraid of not being good enough at something, failing at something or being "found out." Without any effort at all I can recall many fears I've heard from salon owners and stylists hundreds of times.

"I don't conduct education for our team because I have a fear of public speaking. I don't speak well and I get nervous. I'm so afraid that people will think I'm an idiot." **"So I don't offer education, which means I won't fulfill my life long dream of being an educator for my favorite brand."**

"I don't handout my business cards and ask people to come to our salon because I'm afraid people will say no, and I hate rejection." **"So, I don't prospect for new business which means it will take much longer to build my book."**

"I don't ask for referrals because I'm afraid my clients will find out I'm not busy. I don't want them to think I'm not a good stylist." **"So, I don't get many referrals and I have to work harder because I rely on walk-ins."**

"I don't ask for feedback from my clients because, if they're not happy, I won't know how to respond." **"So, I have very low interaction with my clients and I think that is one reason I have low retention numbers."**

"I don't recommend product because I'm afraid clients will think I'm a pushy sales person. I'm their stylist. I want to be their friend not a product pusher." **"So, in my consultations I don't include recommendations that will help them at home, based on my training, education, and experience."**

One of the characteristics of people who leave their mark is their ability to face their fears and continually learn and grow. They have decided that leaving their mark is more important than their limitations. They value their potential enough to take action rather than settle for less. They step outside their comfort zone.

READY TO LEARN

Throughout my career I have used a model to help me understand how people learn—and the conditions that influence how much we learn. In this model there are three areas: The Comfort Zone, The Stretch Zone, and The Panic Zone.

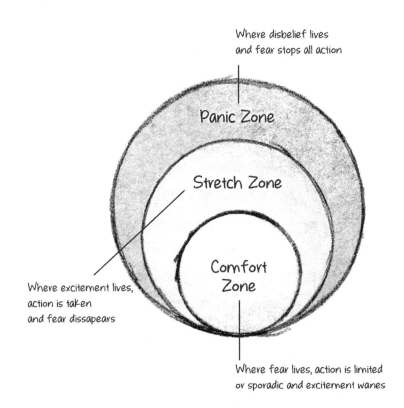

Where disbelief lives and fear stops all action

Panic Zone

Stretch Zone

Comfort Zone

Where excitement lives, action is taken and fear dissapears

Where fear lives, action is limited or sporadic and excitement wanes

THE COMFORT ZONE

Most of us hang out where we're comfortable. The Comfort Zone doesn't push or challenge us physically, mentally, spiritually, emotionally, or psychologically. It is where everything in life is familiar and routine. In times of stress it can be our happy place but, on the downside, there is little or no learning that happens in The Comfort Zone. When we're comfortable, we are not growing and changing and we're not building skills or making progress—at least not very fast. The other thing about The Comfort Zone is that it's where most of our self-centered thinking occurs.

- "I don't want to do that because I may fail."
- "I don't want people to see through me."
- "I don't feel comfortable with that."

In my experience, if you're going to fail, clinging to your comfort zone is a great way to do it. To help you connect with the idea of The Comfort Zone please read these examples. Do you recognize these scenarios?

- Avoiding or refusing to work with "difficult" hair (curly, long, men's, or other types you're not used to).
- Avoiding or refusing to learn how to formulate and work with color.
- Becoming defensive when someone suggests a new approach or gives you feedback.
- Always insisting on "your way" rather than evaluating options or looking at new information.
- Avoiding change and/or being very uncomfortable with it. (Think about how people reacted to the latest salon policy change.)
- Refusing to attend or not paying attention during salon education.

- Never changing your own hairstyle or fashion.
- Not asking for referrals.
- Not recommending product.

THE PANIC ZONE

We usually enter The Panic Zone when we are forced into something that gets us in over our heads, scares us, or is at least very unfamiliar. The Panic Zone overwhelms us with fear and anxiety to the point we can't think straight. When we're forced into this space our "emotional brain" takes over and we go into reaction mode. Compared to the rational part of our brain that helps us think things through, learn, make complex decisions, and manage our thoughts, our emotional brain really hasn't evolved in that way for thousands of years. Our emotional brain is still very important to us but it evolved in ancient times when daily life didn't include lattes, iPhones, and other cool things like, you know, the wheel and fire.

To stress my point, let's take a walk together through a-day-in-the-life of early man. Hugo is out hunting for rodents and berries when, all of a sudden, he feels a warm breath on his back. He whips around to see the giant fangs of a roaring Saber-toothed tiger. At this point, Hugo isn't "thinking logically" about his situation. His emotional brain takes over and puts him on autopilot. He is either going to fight the Saber-toothed tiger to his death or he is going to run like hell and survive. There isn't going to be any decision making or any deep thinking about his options.

The emotional brain helps protect us in these kinds of life-or-death situations. Blood flow is redirected to the arms and legs, while adrenalin rushes into our system, making us ready for "fight or flight." We begin to sweat so we'll be slippery if something does get ahold of us. Our pupils dilate for maximum clarity and concentration.

One of the many problems with our ancient emotional brain is that it can betray us in the modern world. It often tries to take over, even though we don't face that many life-or-death situations, and that can lead to unintended consequences. It also has this inconvenient little defect where it doesn't discriminate between real danger and perceived danger, which causes us to overreact to certain kinds of stimuli. Here's one kind of perceived danger that you may have experienced yourself. Speaking in public.

Year after year the National Institute of Health finds that public speaking is the number one fear of most Americans. Death is number two! Jerry Seinfeld jokes that most people attending funerals would rather be the person in the casket than to stand up and give the eulogy. This is a great example of how our emotional brain causes us to react in ways that aren't helpful. When forced into public speaking most people enter The Panic Zone. You have either seen it or personally experienced the symptoms:

- You stop thinking
- You turn white as a ghost
- You begin to sweat
- You either freeze or run off the stage.

To help you connect with the idea of The Panic Zone see if you recognize yourself, or people on your team, in these examples.

- You finish a color and highlights only to see that your client is visibly upset.
- The salon owner confronts you at the door and demands to know why you're late again.
- A coworker gives you the cold shoulder and won't talk to you for several days.
- You unexpectedly find yourself yelling at the front desk person for double-booking you.

In the last chapter we discussed IQ vs. EQ. One of the earmarks of a highly developed EQ is an ability to understand how you, or someone else, are being controlled by the emotional brain. Being in the Panic Zone is another example where the emotional brain is likely to hijack our ability to think rationally—and that's usually the last place we want to be, especially at work. Recognizing that someone is in their Panic Zone is the first step. Having a plan to help them get out of it is the second step. By the way, yelling, "Calm down!" isn't going to work any better than throwing gasoline on a fire. Once we recognize The Panic Zone we can take a breath and figure out how to help ourselves and others find a more rational place. Here's what we do:

- First acknowledge what's happening rather than ignoring it or pretending it's not happening
- Listen and understand the other person's perception of the situation so you know where he or she is coming from
- Name the emotion you believe is in control to spark a conversation about how they are feeling
- Clarify your intent, and get clarity about the other person's intent, to build the trust you'll need to move forward together
- Create a rational strategy to exit The Panic Zone based on the positive results you want
- Think through ways to learn from the experience, which will shrink your Panic Zone and increase your Stretch Zone.

THE STRETCH ZONE

Unlike The Comfort Zone where you naturally want to hang out, The Stretch Zone is where you should be hanging out—and where you will spend most of your time if you want to leave your mark. Being in The Stretch Zone stimulates personal and professional growth. It's where all the things are that you've always wanted to do, know you should do, but have been afraid to try. The Stretch Zone is where

> *You become a better version of your future self.*

The Stretch Zone has a secret little side benefit. It's where you can access a brain chemical called dopamine. Dopamine is the ultimate pleasure chemical and it is released anytime you accomplish a task, solve a problem, or overcome "the impossible." In other words, the Stretch Zone might not sound like a welcome place at first but, believe me, it feels good.

Another characteristic of The Stretch Zone is that every time you use it, The Comfort Zone gets bigger and The Panic Zone gets smaller! Search your memory (something the rational brain is very good at) for a person you've met who knows all kinds of things, has travelled all over, and seems to be at home in every situation. That is the earmark of a person who inhabits The Stretch Zone a lot.

To help you connect with the idea of The Stretch Zone, see if you recognize yourself, or your people here:

- You have been asked to specialize in men's cuts so you enroll in education to build your skills
- Your clients are not rebooking, so you ask three other stylists for tips to help you improve
- You ask every client how she really feels about her cut, color, and style—and then you listen
- You think it's best to avoid product sales but you keep an open mind about the upcoming prescription pad training class since you may learn something that will shift your thinking
- You decide to put yourself out there by handing out business cards at the gym, the supermarket, your coffee shop, or wherever your type of client hangs out.

EXERCISE

Based on your new knowledge, examine your own behavior and habits. How would you define your zones and which ones are you actively living and working in?

Fill in the blanks to better describe your own Comfort Zone, Panic Zone, and Stretch Zone. When you've finished, ask each member of your team to do this exercise for herself.

ZONE	INTENT
My Comfort Zone	The things I'm most comfortable doing are_____ _____ The new things I'm getting comfortable doing are_____ _____ _____
My Panic Zone	I really panic when I'm forced to _____ _____ _____
My Stretch Zone	What I need to do even more of is _____ _____ _____

Now take the three descriptions you recorded in the table on the prior page and rewrite them in the following table starting in the left-hand column. Once you have that, write a simple action plan to increase your Comfort Zone, Increase your Stretch Zone, and reduce your Panic Zone.

ZONE	ACTION PLAN	DATE
The things I'm most comfortable doing are		
The new things I'm getting comfortable doing are		
I really panic when I'm forced to		
What I need to do even more of is		

Finally, examine this list of common salon experiences and behaviors. Place an X by each one and then describe how you will improve by a specific date.

TOPIC	COMFORT ZONE	PANIC ZONE	STRETCH ZONE	ACTION PLAN	DATE
Personal growth					
Professional growth					
Fashion					
Hair, skin, makeup					
Health and fitness					
Technical skills					
People skills					
Leadership					
Growing your business					
Employee relationships					
Client experience					
Create and support salon culture					
Building your brand					

HOW DO YOU LIKE
ME SO FAR?

There is no failure. Only feedback.

ROBERT ALLEN

I have a magic pill that will instantly make people like you better. They will be more interested in what you have to say, tell you everything you want to know, tell you how they feel about you, and share how they see your performance. Are you interested? This pill will give you the thinking and the skills to get helpful information from people, understand it, and act on it. Finally, my little pill will help you communicate in ways that others can hear, understand, accept, and use.

FEEDBACK

Everything has a life cycle. There is a beginning, middle, and end to everything on Earth. In fact, our Sun is already middle-aged with only about five billion years left to live. I think I've dropped enough hints to let you know I believe in God, but believe me, when the Sun goes, Earth is going with it like a piece of popcorn in a microwave.

People have a life cycle too. We're born, we live, and, well, let's not talk about the rest until we're all a lot older. To continue growing is the secret to extending our happy lives; personally, in relationships, and at work. We all know that plants have a growing season. We plant them in the spring, they grow in the summer, and we harvest them in the fall. (Sorry plants, we get hungry.) People are different. Our season can be extended over and over as long as we are willing to keep growing mentally and emotionally. And the key to growth is feedback.

Feedback is,

> *Perspective that empowers us to see, adjust, and grow throughout our journey.*

LEADERS SET THE TONE

Feedback is just one of the thousands of areas where the rule of "leading by example" applies. As a salon owner, if you ask for feedback, and genuinely consider how it can empower you, your team will pick up on your behavior. If you ask for feedback as a stylist, truly listen, and then adjust and grow, your clients will love you for it and stay with you for a lifetime.

On the other hand, if we shut down, reject feedback, or defend and explain ourselves, others will see it as too painful and useless to try helping us. When you don't receive constructive feedback, you risk being isolated from your team. When you don't give constructive feedback, you are missing opportunities to develop your people to their full potential.

AFRAID TO ASK

Many of us avoid asking for any feedback at all, preferring to stay in our Comfort Zone. Some of us are afraid of what we might hear. Some of us may not think we need any feedback, and for others it just doesn't cross our minds.

Whether we are talking about you, your clients, employees, or personal relationships, giving and receiving feedback is essential to improved performance and satisfaction for everyone in your life. Giving feedback is something you do everyday as an owner or manager—at least you will by the end of this chapter. Anyway, it's not just what you say but also how you let your team know where they are compared to your standards of performance. If they're on the right track, feedback is a great way to encourage them. If they're on the wrong track, it's how you begin to correct performance before it becomes a problem. Either way, feedback helps all of us leave our mark because open, honest, and on-time[1] communication is what helps us grow and improve.

CRAIG HEARD IT RIGHT

Craig was a man that worked for me back when I was a manager at a prominent retailer. I loved working with Craig because I could tell him exactly how I was feeling about his performance on any given task at any given time. He always responded with a smile and thanked me for my feedback. He listened without interrupting. If he didn't agree with me or didn't understand my point he would say, "Tell me more." He never once defended or explained why something happened or why something didn't get done to my satisfaction. I remember kidding him, "You can take a beating better than anyone I have ever met." He would smile and respond, "Why not? You're helping me get better at my job, helping me to be liked better by my peers and my team and ultimately to be more successful and get promoted. What's not to smile about?" Craig would respond the same way whenever a customer had a complaint or one of his employees had an issue. I learned how to receive feedback by watching Craig. He was a natural at it. This was his approach:

- Listen
- Acknowledge
- Ask clarifying questions to better understand
- Avoid being defensive
- Never defend and explain
- Believe that feedback is empowering
- Always say, "Thank you."

ASKING FOR FEEDBACK

Feedback can be solicited (you ask for it) or unsolicited (you don't ask for it but you get it anyway). I recommend you ask for feedback early and often. One reason is that it gives you more control and helps you to be more receptive. In your role at work you want feedback in a timely manner so you can:

- Measure your results more accurately

- Compare your results to what you intended to do
- Improve your plans to get you closer to your goals
- Continue to grow.

Ask for feedback on your performance as close to the activity as possible. Don't wait for hours, days, or weeks to pass. For example, ask for feedback:

- From your manager right after your one-on-one
- From your team right after you introduce a new marketing campaign
- From your clients right after their services
- From your manager right after doing something important for the salon.

DOES THIS STORY MAKE ME LOOK FAT?

One time, right before joining friends for dinner, my wife asked me, "How do I look?" I said, "I think you should put on a different top." She said, "Thanks Mr. Blackwell but I was asking about my hair." Thirty minutes later, when we started speaking again, I told her she may want to be more specific next time to get the feedback she's after. After another hour of silence, I apologized for not asking a clarifying question like, "What specifically are you asking about? Your hair, makeup, wardrobe, or accessories?" This was a great learning moment for me. In addition to learning my wife doesn't fully appreciate my comic genius, I also realized that by asking for specific feedback we improve our chances of getting the feedback we want. By asking clarifying questions we improve our chances of giving relevant feedback.

So, when you ask for feedback it is important to state your question precisely. Avoid general questions like, "How am I doing?" "How did I do?" or, "How was your experience today?"

Instead be specific when you ask for feedback:

Be specific with clients, "How do you like your cut? How do you like your color? How do you like your styling?"
Be specific with your manager, "How well am I living out our salon culture?"
Managers, be specific with your stylists, "How well am I supporting your needs for education?"

It's also very helpful to use a measurement scale to pinpoint where you are. Often a scale from 1-10, where 10 is best, helps people communicate how well they think someone else is doing.

Ask your clients, "On a scale of 1-10, how well do you like your cut today?"
Ask your manager, "On a scale of 1-10, how do you feel I'm doing with client retention?"
Manager asks stylists, "On a scale of 1-10, how well am I communicating our brand on social media?"

NOW YOU'VE DONE IT!

Once you've asked for feedback, and received it, you must acknowledge the other person's feedback and any feelings or emotions that surfaced.

CLIENT: "I hate this color!"
STYLIST ACKNOWLEDGES: "It sounds like you had a different shade in mind."

MANAGER: "I'm not giving you any more walk-ins."
STYLIST ACKNOWLEDGES: "It sounds like you are not comfortable with how I work with new clients."

MANAGER: "You are not fully booked."

STYLIST ACKNOWLEDGES: "It sounds like you have a specific number or goal in mind."

NEVER ASSUME

You've heard it said, "Never assume because it makes an ASS out of U and ME." So, please don't assume you know how another person feels. Ask a clarifying question immediately after acknowledging their feedback to better understand why they are feeling that way. For example:

Clarify with clients, "It sounds like you had a different shade in mind. *Would you show me on the color wheel which red you wanted?*"

Clarify with your manager, "It sounds like you are not comfortable with how I work with new clients. *What should I be doing to earn more walk-ins?*"

Clarify with your manager, "It sounds like you have a specific number or goal in mind. *How many clients do you think I should see on a daily basis?*"

Repeat the process of acknowledging and questioning throughout the conversation until the other person has shared everything. I find it's very helpful to ask, "What else?" until the other person says, "That's all." That's how you'll know when you've gotten to the bottom of the issue.

Acknowledging and questioning is powerful. It lets the other person feel validated and understand you are truly interested in what they have to say. It also paves the way for you to learn more by asking clarifying questions. Do you remember the mirror neuron and how it likes to mirror the behavior of the other person? Remember, the attitude I take with you is likely to be the attitude you will take with me. Therefore, if you defend and explain your behavior, I will defend and explain my reasons why I don't like your behavior. Instead, ask heartfelt clarifying questions and respond openly without being defensive. If you do, the other person is much more likely to respond the same way.

"THANK YOU!"

Because feedback is a tool to help us get better, people who offer feedback are actually giving you a gift. Tell them, "Thank you!" That's the appropriate response when someone gives you a gift. Look the person in the eye (both eyes if you're extra coordinated) and thank them for their time and interest in sharing feedback with you. When you acknowledge their perspective **it doesn't mean you agree with them.** After all, feedback is just information. You're the one who decides which feedback to value and if you can trust it to help you improve and to reach your potential.

GIVING UNSOLICITED FEEDBACK

Unlike Craig's ability to receive feedback, I haven't met many who were gifted at giving feedback to others. Typically, people give feedback that is unwelcome, beats around the bush too much, or that is too difficult to understand. One of the ways I strive to leave my mark is by sharing effective ways to give direct, constructive, and helpful feedback. Here is what I recommend.

GIVING PLACEMENT

Explaining what your feedback is about, known as "giving placement,7" tells the other person exactly what you want to talk about. This eliminates their burden to guess—especially since most of us jump to conclusions and assume the worst. In other words, if you want to give someone feedback about how they can improve their level of trust with their clients, you don't want them wasting emotional energy worrying about whether or not they're getting fired. Another common mistake we make is trying to give too much feedback all at once. I've found it's far more effective to pick one or two issues and make your feedback very focused. If you stack issues on top of each other the receiver gets overwhelmed and shuts down. Here is an example of how giving placement works.

> **SALON OWNER**: "I would like to have a conversation about how to improve your retention numbers."
>
> **STYLIST**: "My retention numbers are fine."
>
> **SALON OWNER**: "I would like to hear more about your expectations for retention and see how those match up with the salon's expectations."

ASK PERMISSION

Beyond the fact that it's just good manners, our brains are wired to enjoy being asked permission. Once you've explained what you want to talk about, ask for permission before you launch into it. As you learn the process for correctly giving and receiving feedback, monitor how you used to do it and then compare it to what you're learning here. I believe it's especially important to listen to yourself during the "permission" phase. Many people are so quick to jump into giving their feedback that the listener gets overwhelmed and defensive from the very start. Here's an example of how to use permission to help you provide better feedback.

> **SALON OWNER**: "I would like to have a conversation today about retention. What times work best for you?"
>
> **STYLIST**: "Honestly, now doesn't work very well since Anna is already here for her appointment."

SALON OWNER: "Ah, good point. When would it be OK to put 15 minutes in your book today?"

STYLIST: "I have an opening from 3:15 to 3:45. Let's meet at 3:15."

STATE YOUR INTENTIONS

Have you ever been in a phone or email conversation and found yourself saying something like, "I'd rather talk about this face-to-face"? We all gain information from body language and non-verbal cues, so the ideal scenario is to be face to face with the other person to better understand them. Whether you're in the same room (which I highly recommend) or on the phone, when you give feedback to someone it's important to focus your attention on the feedback session and to state your intent up front—that way the other person doesn't have to "read" you. By stating your intent they can save their energy for listening. Here's what it looks like.

SALON OWNER: "Before we get started, I want you to know that my intent is to help you by shifting your thinking about the importance of retention as a way for you to become more successful."

STYLIST: "I know you support me and I appreciate it. I'd like to be more successful too."

I realize this is new for many of you, so let's take a second to see where we are at this point in our feedback process:

- We stated what our feedback will be about
- The receiver has given us permission to proceed
- We clearly stated our intent so the receiver understands, "where we're coming from."

GET THE OTHER PERSON'S PERSPECTIVE

Now, before we take the next step, we do something that helps the other person take responsibility and feel a sense of control. It also gives us a chance to collect more information on their thinking and to help fine-tune our feedback as we go along. At this point, we ask the other person for their perspective.

> **SALON OWNER**: "You told me you thought your retention numbers were fine. What do you feel is a good number for retention?"
> **STYLIST**: "I guess I have always thought retention should be 100%. I mean, if clients love me they should all come back, right?"

SHARE YOUR FEEDBACK

I know this sounds like a lot of steps but once you get used to this approach the steps will seem much simpler and become second nature. **In real life it will only take about 90 seconds** to get to this point. And remember, most people give feedback very poorly or incorrectly so no matter how fast they do it they're wasting everyone's time. When feedback is not taken the right way, the other person shuts down, and we lose the opportunity to help them grow.

OK, we're now ready. If done properly, the other person is open and ready to hear what you have to say.

> **SALON OWNER**: "I've heard other stylists tell me the same thing: 100%. I've also heard 50% as being a good number. For perspective, the minimum our best stylists achieve is 65%. I've never seen anyone—myself included—hit more than 80% on a long-term basis. Based on what I shared with you what would be your new thinking?"
> **STYLIST**: "OK. So, I'm at 57%. I need to be thinking about how I can get that number up."

CLARIFY YOUR OBJECTIVE

We want to work together to set the right objective. The idea is for the other person to take responsibility for setting an objective that also meets our needs. In our example, most salon owners would simply give the employee a number to hit. The problem with this approach is that it doesn't really engage the other person. Instead, we want the other person to look thoughtfully at the situation and come up with their own idea. If they can do that, they're much more likely to be emotionally committed and hold themselves accountable with little or no direction from us.

Basically, the idea is to get them to solve the problem in a way that also works for us. It all starts with a question.

> **SALON OWNER:** "Based on the fact you want to get your retention number up, what do you think is realistic number to attain in the next 45 days?"
> **STYLIST:** "In 45 days, I think I can get to 65%".
> **SALON OWNER:** "I like your thinking. What are your ideas on how to get there?"
> **STYLIST:** "I can start with a better consultation. Truthfully, I just need to start doing consultations to better understand my clients' expectations. If I know their expectations then I can meet them."

IDENTIFY SOLUTION AND GAIN COMMITMENT

One day I asked my son, "Hey, I thought you were going to clean your room today?" He replied, "I know that was your expectation but we never agreed on it."

Commitment is a special word in business and it should be a special word in your salon. Someone may understand you—and that is one thing. You may have an expectation that someone will do something, and that is also real. Someone may even agree with you—

and that is another. A commitment, however, is a special step beyond understanding, beyond expectation, and more than an agreement. **It is a promise to do something by a specific date.**

> *"A commitment = what + when."*

SALON OWNER: "What I'm hearing you say is you think doing consultations will lead to higher retention. Is that correct?"

STYLIST: "Yes. That's what I'm thinking."

SALON OWNER: "I like it. How soon will you start these consultations and how many of your clients will receive them?"

STYLIST: "Well, it's going to take some getting used to but I can start by next week."

SALON OWNER: "Great! Which day next week are you committing to start consultations and how many of your clients will you provide consultations for?"

STYLIST: "I commit to providing consultations to each of my clients starting next Tuesday."

STATE YOUR SUPPORT

Encourage your people by showing your support for their new commitment—as well as being there to help them stay on track.

SALON OWNER: "I appreciate how receptive you've been to my feedback and this process. I'm here to support you and help you to see this through. Please let me know what more I can do."

STYLIST: "That makes me feel better. How do other stylists go about consultations when they haven't been doing them? I don't want it to feel awkward for my clients or for me."

SALON OWNER: "Jenny has the top retention numbers. What are your thoughts about speaking with her about how she does consultations and how soon could you do that?"

STYLIST: "She and I are good friends. I'll ask her in the break room today."

SUMMARIZE UNDERSTANDINGS

The final step is to summarize what just happened so that you are completely on the same page with the other person.

SALON OWNER: "I have some notes about our conversation. I'll email them to you to make sure we honor our agreements and our commitments."

STYLIST: "That sounds great. I took notes too. I'll send you mine."

SALON OWNER: "I appreciate that. I know your clients will be more loyal and trusting, your retention will improve, and I feel good about your commitment."

WHEN IS FEEDBACK APPROPRIATE?

As they say, "There is more than one way to skin a cat." That is one of the enormous benefits of diversity in the workplace. Different people have different experiences, skills, and gifts and we want to help each one flourish. That's why I advocate letting people pursue their strengths—which let's me be a cheerleader as I offer words of encouragement while I watch people doing things they love. My favorite time to give feedback is anytime something is going well—especially when it could be going even better. *I love coaching the other person to bring out their best in areas they are already strong.*

When feedback is needed because of a missed expectation, or someone falls short of the standards you set, try to limit your feedback to the following six areas of improvement. Too much feedback can be a very bad thing when it leads to feelings of oppression and micromanagement. Don't try to control everything through excessive feedback. It may seem like a legitimate thing to do but, in reality, it just doesn't work that way.

THE SIX AREAS OF IMPROVEMENT

1. When clients are dissatisfied with one or more of us.
2. When our brand as a salon is negatively impacted.
3. When something is not going according to plan.
4. Performance or quality standards are not being met.
5. Revenue or profit targets are missed.
6. Culture issues, team member issues, or conflicts go unresolved.

SIMPLE DO'S AND DON'TS

Even if we limit ourselves to giving feedback to just six categories, there are still a lot of things that pop up where feedback is warranted. Here is a simple list of do's and don'ts to help you get the idea how your choice of language impacts the other person's ability to hear, understand, accept, and act on what you're telling them.

Continue to exercise on the next page.

DO SAY	DON'T SAY
I want you to be successful.	You're not meeting expectations.
I want to give you constructive feedback on...	Let me tell you what you are doing wrong...
I want to help you...	Someone told me...
I would like to help you listen with an open mind.	Don't be defensive.
I'd like this to be the last time we have to address this issue.	You'd better...
I want to build a strong culture that includes you.	You're not a team player.
I want to create a harmonious environment that both clients and stylists love.	None of your clients or coworkers like you.
What would you tell me about...?	I heard from someone on the team who heard from a coworker...
How important is this to you on a scale of 1-10?	This is obviously not important to you...
What is your perspective?	Let me tell you what happened...
I felt...when you did or said...	You were rude, mean, or sarcastic.
What has changed for you since the beginning of this conversation?	You're contradicting what you said at the beginning of the conversation.
Of the several points you mentioned, which point would you start with?	You're all over the place with your thinking.
How can I help you think through this?	You've got to figure this out on your own.
What questions do you have?	Are we done here?
I want this to work. I am committed. How committed are you?	I don't know if you can do this but we can try.
Here is what we've agreed to...	Here's what I want to happen...

EXERCISES

Are you ready to give and receive constructive feedback to help yourself and others with perspectives that empower us to see, adjust, and grow throughout our journeys? Do these exercises and you'll feel the confidence to give it a try.

ASKING FOR FEEDBACK

Remember, we ask for feedback early and often. The more we do it the easier it becomes. The more feedback we receive the more information we have to make adjustments and improvements to our mental and emotional growth. Here are a few examples to cement the idea. Follow through by filling in the blanks to create your own personalized approach to asking for feedback.

(*Continue to exercise on the next page*).

TOPIC	HOW TO START OFF	ACKNOWLEDGE	CLARIFY
Clients	I would love to get some feedback. On a scale of 1-10 how do you like your hairstyle?	So, what I'm hearing is that your 7 means we could have done better.	What would you like to see change?
Employees	I would like to get your feedback on what it's like to work here. What would you share with me?	When I hear, "It's OK" I realize I could be making this a better place to work for you.	What are two thing we could do to make it better than OK?

		How am I as a coworker?	You said, "Most of the time you're a blast to work with." That just made my day.	What would you share with me about the times I'm not so great to work with?			
Employees							
Peers							

OFFERING FEEDBACK

When someone asks you for feedback, I want you to think, "I am about to empower this person." When someone needs feedback, but doesn't ask for it, I want you to think, "How can I do this so this person will hear it as empowering and use it as input for their personal or professional growth?"

The next table summarizes the key points you just learned about giving unsolicited feedback. The one after that gives you some blank space to use the next time you're providing feedback to someone.

Continue to exercise on the next page.

STEPS TO GIVING FEEDBACK	KEY PHRASES
Give placement	"I would like to have a conversation about how to improve your retention numbers."
Ask permission	"I would like to have a conversation today about retention. What times work best for you?"
State intent	"Before we get started, I want you to know that my intent is to help you by shifting your thinking about the importance of retention as a way for you to become more successful."
Get their perspective	"What is your retention number and what do you feel is a good number for retention in general?"
Share your feedback	"To give perspective, the minimum our best stylists achieve is 65%. I've never seen anyone –myself included –hit more than 80% on a long-term basis. Based on what I shared with you what would be your new thinking?"
Clarify your objective	"Based on the fact you want to get your number up, what do you think is realistic in the next 45 days?"
Identify solution & gain commitment	"Which day next week are you committing to start consultations and how many of your clients will you provide consultations for?"
State your support	"I'm here to support you and help you see this through."
Summarize mutual understanding	"I have some notes about our conversation. I'll email them to you to make sure we honor our agreements and our commitments."

Here's your blank template to use in future feedback sessions.

DATE: _____

NAME: _____

STEPS TO GIVING FEEDBACK	IN YOUR OWN WORDS
Give placement	
Ask permission	
State intent	
Get their perspective	
Share your feedback	
Clarify your objective	
Identify solution & gain commitment	
State your support	
Summarize mutual understanding	

CONCLUSION

Knowing is not enough, we must apply.
Willing is not enough, we must do.

BRUCE LEE

After meeting thousands of salon owners, and many thousands of stylists, I am happy to say how endlessly fascinated I am by our industry. One of my fascinations is about who we are as artists and how we express our art. Of course there are exceptions but, in general, stylists are *commercial* artists. That is, while you may also be a painter or sculptor making art for its own sake, when you work with people and hair, you're doing it to make a living.

It was very much like that for me when I set out to write this book. My intention was to concentrate the most essential thinking, behaviors, and people skills into *Leave Your Mark* as I possibly could because the psychology of working with and leading people is *my art*. So, it won't be much of a surprise to learn that I don't want to just show you my art for it's own sake—my work will not be complete until you put *Leave Your Mark* into action in your personal and professional life.

In the Introduction, I said the **purpose of this book** is to convince you that leaving your mark is the most important thing you will ever do and **the value of this book** is to shift your thinking. Both of these ideas only have meaning if you take what you've learned here and

Do something about it!

There is an entire field of research, and volumes of books, dedicated to the studies of human motivation, decision making, and creating new habits. Here, again, what I hope to do is give you the essential information to go from where you are (armed with new thinking, behaviors, and people skills) and take you to where you need to be (using this new information to become a better salon owner, a better stylist, and a better person).

So, what do we know about what it takes to make something new happen? Well, let's break it down—using you, as a salon owner, as the example. (We can do the same thing with "You as a stylist." Make sure to ask me about that perspective at an upcoming workshop or by email. My contact information is included in the final few pages.)

Original situation. You're a salon owner now, but go back with me to when you were a stylist. There was something going on in your original situation that I'm sure you remember like it was yesterday. There was some kind of hunger. It may have been a hunger for more creative control, to make more money, to have more influence, or to get out of a toxic salon environment. Whatever it was, in your original situation, you were not satisfied and you were hungry for something. What was it? Write down your original situation here:

_____

_____

_____

_____

_____

Vision. Back in your original situation, you started to dream of a future where things would be different. It was probably fuzzy at first but before long you came up with a creative name, an approach to client service, an interior layout and design, and even the kind of people you would hire to help you realize your dream of creating a salon the way it should be. One step at a time you developed your vision. It's probably very similar to the vision you still have today. What is your vision for your salon? Write down your vision here:

_____

_____

_____

_____

_____

Reward. Injected somewhere between your original situation and your vision was a reward, or a set of rewards, that you knew were worth making sacrifices for. You knew that even if you had to work longer hours, take on some financial risk, ask friends and family for help, and then scrimp and save, that those rewards were worth having—no matter what. What were the rewards you thought were worth all the effort back then? Write down your rewards here:

Commitment. After a lot of thought, and probably a lot of second-guessing yourself, you took a step that marked the point of no return: You told someone about your dream. A funny thing happens when you share your dreams with another person. They say, "It's a lot easier to let the cat out of the bag than to put it back in." So, once you let it slip that you were thinking about opening your own salon, people started to expect you to do it! One of the best ways to make a commitment to yourself is to tell someone else about it. How did you work up the courage to make the commitment to opening your own salon? Who did you let in on your dream? Write down how you made your commitment here:

Planning. By then it was becoming clear to you that you were actually going to go for it and open your own salon. But, as you learned, your salon wasn't going to open itself so you started putting plans in place to make it happen. That's one of the most beautiful things about salon owners—they know how to make stuff happen! You thought about timing, income, investment, locations, suppliers, clients, staff, and a thousand other things. If you're like most people, you didn't think of everything in advance but, in the end, you had a plan. Looking back on it, what would you say your plan was? Write down the highlights of your plan here:

_____

_____

_____

_____

_____

Taking the First Step. Up to a certain point, your vision was just a pipe dream. All the planning in the world wouldn't have added up to much more than pleasant thoughts if you hadn't taken your first step. Not that I'm in favor of it, but the first step for some of you may have been to up and quit your old job. Others may have raised the money needed for the investment as their first step. Still others, may have signed a lease on, "The perfect location," even though they had no idea how to make the first payment. Whatever it was, what was your first step? Write down the story of your first step here:

_____

_____

_____

_____

_____

Have you ever been to one of those amusement parks where trained animals do the most amazing tricks? Dancing bears, balancing elephants, dogs riding bikes, and killer whales—well, that's probably enough of that. Anyway, do you know how they learn to do those complicated behaviors? Their trainers start by getting them to do something they either already know how to do or that they already do naturally. Now, I might not know your natural talents but I already know that you can put into action the thinking, behaviors, and people skills in this book.

How do I know that? Because I trust you. After all, you just wrote down the story of how you opened your salon—and that was among the hardest things you've ever done. If you use the same process you used to open your salon, and focus it on implementing the ideas in this book, then I am certain you can leave your mark. Here's how.

Original Situation>Vision>Reward>Commitment>Planning>First Step

Original situation. If you think about your leadership skills and people skills, and if you're like 99% of people on the planet, you could probably be doing better. I admit that I can't magically give you the hunger, but if you have the hunger to be a better leader and a better person, then write down your original situation here. Describe your strengths and weaknesses as a people person and as a leader (reflecting on the chapters in this book):

_____

_____

_____

_____

_____

Vision. Now, where do you want to be as a leader and as a person? What is your vision for the leader you could become and for the people your team could become? Write down your vision here:

_____

_____

_____

_____

_____

Reward. Look, there has to be something very desirable in this for you if you're going to put all of this into action. I can spend hours telling you *the rewards I think you should want* but there has to be something you, personally, really really want. Otherwise, none of this will go anywhere. Can you write down the rewards you are willing to make sacrifices for?

_____

_____

_____

_____

_____

Commitment. In the chapter, "Giving and Receiving Feedback," we defined commitment as a promise to do something by a specific date. What are you willing to promise yourself? Are you ready to leave your mark on your business and the people in your personal and professional life? Write down what you are promising to do and when you will make it happen. Write down who you are going to tell. That person(s) is the one who will share in your commitment and has your permission to hold you accountable.

_____

_____

_____

_____

_____

Planning. Looking back on how you opened your salon, I'm willing to bet that you now think you could have done a better job of planning. A good plan doesn't have to be super long. It just has to address all the steps to take you from point A to point B. Lucky for you! Every chapter in this book laid out steps to go from point A and point B. Within every chapter was an exercise. Each of those exercises encouraged you to take specific action. No matter what your final plan looks like, rely on those exercises to jump-start your planning. Write down the highlights of your plan here:

_____

_____

_____

_____

_____

Taking the First Step. You are about to finish reading this book. The question you need to ask yourself: "Is this the end of this book or the beginning of a new journey on the way to leaving my mark?" The distance between putting this book down and putting it to work will be defined by a choice you are already in the process of making. If I never get to meet you, or if I never get to see you again, and I could only say one thing that I honestly think can change your life, this is it:

Write down your first step (and then take it!):

_____

_____

_____

_____

_____

NOTES

1. Stan Slap, "Bury My Heart In Conference Room B: The Unbeatable Impact of Truly Committed Managers." Penguin, 2010.

2. "Values Development." http://changingminds.org/explanations/values/values_development.htm Quoting Morris Massey. Retrieved September 8, 2016.

3. Stephen R. Covey, Rebecca R. Merrill, "The SPEED of Trust: The One Thing That Changes Everything." Free Press, 2006.

4. "Increasing Your Salary with Emotional Intelligence." http://www.talentsmart.com/articles/Increasing-Your-Salary-With-Emotional-Intelligence-983916766-p-1.html by Dr. Travis Bradberry & Nick Tasler, M.S. Retreived September 8, 2016.

5. Travis Bradberry and Jean Greaves, "Emotional Intelligence 2.0" TalentSmart, 2009.

6. Daniel H. Pink, "Drive: The Surprising Truth About What Motivates Us." Riverhead Books, 2009.

7. David Rock, "Quiet Leadership: Six Steps to Transforming Performance at Work." HarperCollins, 2006.

ABOUT THE AUTHOR

Thirty-five years of experiences give you an amazing perspective. It taught me to see all of us as people filled with possibilities. We have an internal engine that can propel abilities beyond circumstance. Beyond excuses. Beyond negativism. Beyond the ordinary. In order to leave my mark I start with this truth in mind and then help people surprise their world with what they already possess. My passion is to help transform people, to give them hope, kindle their motivation, to unlock possibilities, and offer change that is sustainable. Finally, to put them on a path to lead their every endeavor. I am a husband, father, leader, coach, engager, knowledge opener, change seeker, and a friend who wants to leave my mark—by helping you to leave yours.

CONTACT THE AUTHOR

I'm always thrilled to hear from you and to learn what's on your mind. Whether you have a comment, a question, or encouragement you can reach me here: jay@jaywilliamsco.com.